Be Transformed

HOMEWORK ONLY EDITION

Discovering Biblical Solutions
to Life's Problems

A Discovery Group Study Series presented by Scope Ministries International

International Standard Book Number
ISBN
9781470013554
Library of Congress Catalogue Number

Scriptural quotations are from the following versions of the Bible indicated as follows:

Amplified Bible Expanded Edition	(Amplified)
The Living Bible	(LB)
New American Standard Bible	(NAS)
New International Version of the Bible	(NIV)
New Testament in Modern English by J.B. Phillips	(Phillips)

Any reference to Bibical Personal Guidance Ministry, or One-on-One Ministry are one in the same.

About The Cover

The theme of the cover is based on the word pictures given by the prophet Jeremiah and Jesus in the following passages:

Blessed is the man who trusts in the Lord and whose trust is the Lord. For he will be like a tree planted by the water, that extends its roots by a stream and will not fear when the heat comes; but its leaves will be green, and it will not be anxious in a year of drought nor cease to yield fruit. Jeremiah 17:7-8 NAS

"If any man is thirsty, let him come to Me and drink. He who believes in Me, as the Scripture said, *'From his innermost being shall flow rivers of living water.'*" John 7:37b-38

Scope uses the tree to represent man's three-part nature: spirit, soul, and body.

- The roots of the tree represent the *spirit* of man, which is the means of knowing and worshipping God.

- The trunk represents man's *soul*, the means of expressing the mind, will, and emotions.

- The leaves represent the *body*, the most noticeable and changing aspect of man and the means of doing.

- The sky depicts the wind of God's Spirit at work in the world.

- The river of living water is the Holy Spirit indwelling the believer's spirit (roots), filling the soul (trunk) and producing fruit in the body (leaves).

- The roots of the tree are rooted in God's love and are one with Christ's Spirit.

- The believer is drinking from the river of life and being filled with the Holy Spirit.

- The leaves of the tree pointed upward are depicting a life of worship and praise.

- Jesus is visible in the tree, reproducing His life in the soul (trunk) and expressing Himself through the body (leaves).

Discovering the Root of Our Problems - Day One

Goal: To identify the problem from your perspective and to ask God to reveal His perspective of the problem.

All of us experience problems. Life is full of problems. Success is not the absence of problems but knowing how to respond and resolve the problems. God has not left us alone to try to overcome our problems in our own strength and wisdom. He has given us the Holy Spirit and His Word to empower and teach us.

> Every Scripture is God-breathed (given by His inspiration) and profitable for instruction, for reproof *and* conviction of sin, for correction of error *and* discipline in obedience, [and] for training in righteousness (in holy living, in conformity to God's will in thought, purpose, and action), so that the man of God may be complete *and* proficient, well-fitted *and* thoroughly equipped for every good work.   II Timothy 3:16-17 Amplified

These verses tell us that God's Word is sufficient and profitable to make us adequate and equipped. In other words, God's Word shows us the way or path to abundant living (teaching). God's Word shows us when we get off the path (reproof). God's Word shows us how to get back on the path (correction) and how to stay on the path (training in righteousness). This path is not merely a set of correct behaviors we are to perform. God is committed to showing us when we leave the path of correct beliefs and thoughts as well as correcting our behavior.

1. What problem(s) do you want God to change or address in your life? (conflict in relationship, emotional struggle, habit, or behavior)

2. How is this problem affecting you emotionally?

3. What behaviors or habits in your life are contributing to this problem?

4. How is your behavior affecting your relationships with others?

5. What are some prevailing thoughts that run through your mind when you think about your unique problem?

6. How do you see your problem affecting your relationship with God?

In time, as you seek God's perspective, you will be able to recognize the beliefs that are contributing to these problems and replace those beliefs with the truth as revealed in God's Word.

7. Write your prayer, asking God to begin showing you His perspective of your problem(s) and any beliefs that are contributing to it.

Discovering the Root of Our Problems - Day Two

Goal: To see from Scripture the effect our beliefs have on our lives.

Part One: Because we are believing beings, we each create a belief system that controls our lives. Our beliefs are corrupted because they were formed while we were spiritually separated from God and because we were born into a world corrupted by sin.

Read the account of the fall in Genesis 2:8-9, 16-17; 3:1-7.

1. What did God tell Adam in Genesis 2:16-17?

2. What did Satan imply by his question in Genesis 3:1?

3. What subtle lie did Satan use to tempt Eve to doubt what is true? (see Genesis 3:4)

4. Whom did Eve believe?

5. How did her belief affect her behavior? What were the consequences?

6. What do you think is Satan's role in forming people's beliefs today?

7. How has the fall of man affected you personally?

Part Two:

8. The purpose of this short Bible study is to reveal how our beliefs affect our emotions and behavior. Read each passage and write out the resulting emotion and behavior:

Person(s)	Belief	Emotion	Behavior
The Ten Spies Numbers 13:1-2, 17, 20, 23-33	believed they were small and weak	Fear and inadequacy	gave bad report; unwilling to enter the Promised Land; wanted to stone Joshua, Caleb
Joshua and Caleb Numbers 13:1-2, 17, 20, 23-33	believed God had given them the land and would give them the ability to take possession		
Moses Exodus 4:10-15	believed he was inadequate		
Disciples Mark 4:35-41	believed they were perishing		
Jesus	believed His heavenly Father was in control		

9. What conclusions can you draw from these examples?

   On what was each behavior based?

10. How do your beliefs compare with those in the examples above?

11. Write out a prayer asking God to reveal to you the truth from His Word.

Discovering the Root of Our Problems - Day Three

Goal: To begin uncovering some of your basic life beliefs.

Part One:

1. Complete the following sentences with the first answer that comes to your mind:

   I would be more successful if...

   I would be happier if...

   I could never be happy if...

   I would feel more secure if...

   I would be more peaceful if...

2. What beliefs are revealed by your answers?

Part Two:

3. Choose one of your beliefs revealed in question 2 and write out your corresponding thoughts, emotions, and behaviors. See the examples below:

> EXAMPLE #1:
> Belief: Making a lot of money means I am successful.
> Thoughts: Consumed with getting ahead, bigger house, better car, etc.
> Emotions: Feel anxious about job; angry at co-workers who seem to block goals; envious of co-workers' success; guilt
> Behavior: Workaholic, drink to relieve stress from job, not spending time with family, critical of others
>
> EXAMPLE #2:
> Belief: If my spouse would change, I'd be happy.
> Thoughts: "If only he/she would . . ."
>   "Why can't he/she be more like _____'s spouse?"
>   "I'm stuck for life. This marriage is hopeless."
>   "I could never be happy married to this person."
> Emotions: Anger, hurt, rejection, resentment, revenge
> Behavior: Manipulating, nagging, withdrawing, withholding affection, demanding

Belief:

Thoughts:

Emotions:

Behavior:

Discovering the Root of Our Problems - Day Four

Goal: To see from God's Word how corrupted our minds were when our beliefs
      were formed.

1. According to the following verse, how does Paul describe the thinking of
   an unbeliever?

> You walk no longer just as the Gentiles [unbelievers] also walk, in the futility of their mind
> [foolish and vain thinking], being darkened in their understanding [distorted reasoning],
> excluded [alienated] from the life of God, because of the ignorance that is in them...
> Ephesians 4:17b-18a NAS

2. What knowledge did man feel it was unnecessary to retain?

> And so, since they did not see fit to acknowledge God or approve of Him or consider
> Him worth the knowing, God gave them over to a base [depraved] and condemned
> mind to do things not proper or decent but loathsome, until they were filled (permeated
> and saturated) with every kind of unrighteousness . . .   Romans 1:28-29a Amplified

3. What kind of thinking did God allow to control man?

4. What knowledge do unbelievers now have?

> For the god of this world has blinded the unbelievers' minds [that they should not
> discern the truth], preventing them from seeing the illuminating light of the Gospel of the
> glory of Christ (the Messiah), Who is the Image and Likeness of God.
> II Corinthians 4:4 Amplified

5. On what do their minds focus?

> . . . whose end is destruction (eternal misery), whose god is *their* appetite, and *whose* glory is in their shame, who set their minds on earthly things.   Philippians 3:19b NAS

6. What can you conclude about the thoughts of the unsaved mind?

Note: This does not mean that every thought of man is totally disgusting, vulgar, and repulsive; however, the end result of wrong thoughts is corruption and the exclusion of God.

> Search me, O God, and know my heart; try me and know my anxious thoughts; and see if there be any hurtful way in me, and lead me in the everlasting way.
> Psalm 139:23-24 NAS

7. Take a moment to reflect on the above verse and to ask God to show you any anxious or hurtful thoughts that need to be rejected and replaced with God's truth. Write down any thoughts He shows you.

8. Write Romans 12:2 on a 3x5 card or a post-it note and place it in a prominent place where you will see it often. Each time you see this verse, personalize it as a prayer.

Sample prayer:

Father, I no longer want to be conformed to the thinking of this world. I desire to be transformed by the renewing of my mind. Make me more aware of what I am thinking and show me the lies that I have been believing. I want to live out Your will, which is good, acceptable, and perfect.

Discovering the Root of Our Problems - Day Five

Goal: To continue to identify some of your unique personal beliefs.

Part One: Review

Our beliefs are shaped by our perceptions which are based on our experiences with our parents, family, school, peers, etc.

Scripture clearly states that all are born captive to sin and ignorant of Truth.

> For the wrath of God is revealed from heaven against all ungodliness and unrighteousness of men, who suppress the truth in unrighteousness. Romans 1:18 NAS

> There is none righteous, not even one; There is none who understands, There is none who seeks for God. Romans 3:10b-11 NAS

> For all have sinned and fall short of the glory of God. Romans 3:23 NAS

Growing up in a fallen world, we learn about life from our environment, experiences, and what others teach us. We learn:

- Who we are;
- Whom we can trust;
- What is good or bad;
- What we are worth;
- What our purpose is in life; and
- What God is like.

What we learn becomes our belief system by which we evaluate all new information. We accept or reject new information based on our basic life beliefs. These beliefs are like a lens through which we see life and which control our behavior.

Because our perceptions are distorted and the way we process information is distorted, many of our patterns of behaving and relating to others are also distorted. As others respond to our behavior, their reactions tend to reinforce what we believe to be true.

Part Two: Application

1. Name one significant negative life experience that has shaped what you believe about yourself.

2. List the beliefs formed from that life experience:

   Who am I?

   Whom can I trust?

   What is good or bad?

   What am I worth?

   What is my purpose in life?

3. How have these beliefs been reinforced over the years?

   > Example: Growing up I was poor at math and my dad called me stupid. Kids at school would make fun of me. I hated math all through school and flunked Algebra. I chose not to go to college. I feel like such a failure but I'm afraid to try anything else. Everyone else in my family has a college degree. My dad has never indicated that he is proud of me. Now I find myself being hard on my children when they don't make A's.

4. How are these beliefs still manifested in your thoughts, emotions, behaviors, and relationships? (In other words, how do these beliefs control you? In what areas do you feel held back because of these beliefs?)

   > And I (Jesus) will ask the Father, and He will give you another Helper, that He may be with you forever; *that is* the Spirit of truth whom the world cannot receive, because it does not behold Him or know Him, *but* you know Him because He abides with you, and will be in you . . . But when He, the Spirit of truth, comes, He will guide you into all the truth.
   >   John 14:16-17 NAS

5. Write out a prayer, asking the Holy Spirit to reveal the truth to you concerning these beliefs.

Discovering the Root of Our Problems - Lesson One

Name _____ Date _____

Answer the following questions. To turn in page to small group leader, use identical perforated page in back of book.

1. Briefly describe from DAY ONE the problem with which you are presently struggling.

2. What are some of your "beliefs" that relate to your area of struggle?

3. How are these beliefs affecting you (emotionally, relationally, behaviorally)?

4. What is God showing you from this week's lesson?

5. How often do you turn to God's Word for answers to your problems?
   ___never   ___seldom   ___often   ___ very often   ___ always

6. What questions do you have concerning this week's assignment?

7. Mark the graph to indicate how much of this week's assignment you completed.

None	50%	100%

Record Your Prayer Requests:

Understanding the Good News - Day One

Goal: To recognize your present view of God and how this has affected your understanding of the "good news."

1. Until now, what has been your understanding of the Gospel?

2. Read the lesson and then write a definition of the "good news."

3. Think of a recent time when you were really disappointed with your behavior, and with this in mind, complete the following statements:

   When God thinks about me, He is . . .

   God expects me to . . .

   God is angry with me when I . . .

   God would be more pleased with me if I . . .

   The one thing that frightens me most about God is . . .

4. Based on your answers from question 3, write a description of how you think God views you when you fail.

   Example: "When God thinks about me, He gets angry." This might reveal a belief that God has not forgiven you.

5. What misunderstanding of the "good news" is reflected by your answers in questions 3 and 4?

   Example: Believing God is unforgiving reveals a misunderstanding of God's total forgiveness of your sins.

6. Your answers may be an example of how your concept of God has been distorted as a result of being born separated from God. Look back at this lesson and find a Scripture that corrects your distorted view of God and the Gospel. Based on this verse, write a prayer to God expressing thanks for this "good news."

Understanding the Good News - Day Two

Goal: To understand how God responds to you when you sin.

1. Read John 8:3-11, observing the woman's behavior and Jesus' response.

   a. What was the woman's behavior?

   b. What was Jesus' response to her?

2. Read Luke 15:11-24. The father in this parable represents God, and the two sons represent two types of people.

   a. What was the younger son's behavior?

   b. What was the father's response to the younger son?

   c. What did the son do to get his father's forgiveness?

3. Based on the above examples, how does God respond to you when you sin?

4. Besides forgiving, what else is revealed about God's character in the above passages?

5. How would viewing God this way affect the way you relate to Him in your present situation?

6. Write a prayer expressing to God your desire to experience Him in this way.

Understanding the Good News - Day Three

Goal: To understand more accurately from Scripture the total forgiveness God extends
to you.

Knowing and enjoying God's forgiveness is imperative to a healthy Christian life. What incredible joy it brings when we realize what God has done about our sin. We can now come confidently into His presence with the assurance that our sins are not only forgiven—but forgotten! Based on Hebrews 10, God not only forgives, but forgets our sins and transgressions. What this means is that God will never throw our previous sins back in our faces.

1. What sins have you felt God is still holding against you?

2. Read each verse below and write down what God is communicating to you about His forgiveness, personalizing your answers.

> You were dead in sins, and your sinful desires were not yet cut away. Then He gave you a share in the very life of Christ, for He forgave all your sins, and blotted out the charges proved against you, the list of his commandments which you had not obeyed. He took this list of sins and destroyed it by nailing it to Christ's cross.
>
> Colossians 2:13-14 LB

> The Lord your God is in the midst of you, a Mighty One, a Savior [Who saves]! He will rejoice over you with joy . . . *and* in His love He will be silent *and* make no mention [of past sins, or even recall them]; He will exalt over you with singing.
>
> Zephaniah 3:17 Amplified

> As far as the east is from the west, so far has He removed our transgressions from us.
>
> Psalm 103:12 NAS

> I, even I, am He Who blots out *and* cancels your transgressions, for My own sake, and I will not remember your sins.
>
> Isaiah 43:25 Amplified

> Therefore,[there is] now no condemnation (no adjudging guilty of wrong) for those who are in Christ Jesus. . .
>
> Romans 8:1a Amplified

3. Based on these verses, how many of your sins has God forgiven? Remember, Jesus died for all the sins of the whole world. That means He has already paid for all your future sins as well.

4. Write a note to God thanking Him for His complete forgiveness.

Understanding the Good News - Day Four

Goal: To understand more fully the free gift of eternal life.

1. When you became a Christian, what did you receive?

2. According to the following verse, how does one receive eternal life?

> I assure you, most solemnly I tell you, the person whose ears are open to My words [who listens to My message] and believes *and* trusts in *and* clings to *and* relies on Him Who sent Me has (possesses now) eternal life. And he does not come into judgment [does not incur sentence of judgment, will not come under condemnation], but he has already passed over out of death into life.
>
> John 5:24 Amplified

Often we think of eternal life as merely living forever after death (future) instead of something we receive at salvation and can experience now.

The word "life" is the Greek word *zoe* which refers to the principle of life in the spirit and soul (as opposed to life in the body). *Zoe* represents the highest and best, which Christ is and which He gives to those who believe in Him. It is God's quality of life, which is given to His children. We can better experience *zoe*, God's quality of life, the more we know, perceive, recognize, become acquainted with, and understand God as He really is.

3. Remembering the above definition, read the following verses and write below your observations concerning "eternal life."

> In order that everyone who believes in Him [who cleaves to Him, trusts Him, and relies on Him] may *not perish, but* have eternal life *and* [actually] live forever! For God so greatly loved *and* dearly prized the world, that He [even] gave up His only begotten (unique) Son, so that whoever believes in (trusts in, clings to, relies on) Him shall not perish (come to destruction, be lost) but have eternal (everlasting) life.
>
> John 3:15-16 Amplified

The thief (Satan) comes only in order to steal and kill and destroy. I (Jesus) came that they may have *and* enjoy life, and have it in abundance (to the full, till it overflows).

John 10:10 Amplified

For this is My Father's will *and* His purpose, that everyone who sees the Son and believes in *and* cleaves to *and* trusts in *and* relies on Him should have eternal life, and I will raise Him up [from the dead] at the last day. I assure you, most solemnly I tell you, he who believes *in Me* [who adheres to, trusts in, relies on and has faith in Me] has (now possesses) eternal life.

John 6:40,47 Amplified

I write this to you who believe in (adhere to, trust in, and rely on) the name of the Son of God [in the peculiar services and blessings conferred by Him on men], so that you may know [with settled and absolute knowledge] that you [already] have life, yes, eternal life.

I John 5:13 Amplified

4. What new understanding do these verses give you concerning "eternal life"?

5. God is eternal life, the source of all life. Apart from Him there is no real life. He has chosen to give His life to those who will believe, and who receive Jesus' offer of forgiveness and eternal life. If you have never personally received Jesus as your life you may do this now by simply taking Him at His word and accepting the gift of His life.

But to as many as did receive *and* welcome Him, He gave the authority (power, privilege, right) to become the children of God, that is, to those who believe in (adhere to, trust in, and rely on) His name.

John 1:12 Amplified

Understanding the Good News - Day Five

Goal: To learn how the "good news" applies to your daily life.

1. Eternal life is not just longevity of life but God's quality of life that is to be experienced now, in the midst of life's problems. How does this give you hope in your situation?

2. How would believing that God has completely forgiven you, unconditionally loves you, and totally accepts you change the way you relate to God when you sin?

3. Eternal life is experienced through knowing, recognizing, and becoming acquainted with God (John 17:3). We can experience God's quality of life because Christ died so that we can live.

> For if while we were enemies we were reconciled to God through the death of His Son, much more, having been reconciled, we shall be saved by His life (in us).
>
> Romans 5:10 NAS

Our salvation is not merely an event in our past, but it is to be our ongoing daily experience. As we call upon Jesus in the midst of life's problems, we can experience God's power to deliver us from the bondage of sin.

Salvation is the present experience of God's power to deliver from the bondage of sin. In what areas of your life do you need to experience Christ's deliverance from sin? (See definition of "sin" on 2.4.)

4. Read the following verses and under each one write, in your own words, God's promise to you in your present situation.

> For I am persuaded beyond doubt (am sure) that neither death nor life, nor angels nor principalities, nor things impending *and* threatening nor things to come, nor powers, nor height nor depth, nor anything else in all creation will be able to separate us from the love of God which is in Christ Jesus our Lord.   Romans 8:38-39 Amplified

Example: There is nothing from my past or in my present or in my future that will cause God to stop loving me.

> For He [God] Himself has said, I will not in any way fail you *nor* give you up *nor* leave you without support. [I will] not, [I will] not, [I will] not in any degree leave you helpless *nor* forsake *nor* let [you] down (relax My hold on you)! [Assuredly not!]
> Hebrews 13:5b Amplified

> Do not fear, for I am with you; do not anxiously look about you, for I am your God. I will strengthen you, surely I will help you, surely I will uphold you with My righteous right hand.   Isaiah 41:10 NAS

> [Not in your own strength] for it is God Who is all the while effectually at work in you [energizing and creating in you the power and desire], both to will and to work for His good pleasure *and* satisfaction *and* delight.   Philippians 2:13 Amplified

> And I am convinced *and* sure of this very thing, that He Who began a good work in you will continue until the day of Jesus Christ [right up to the time of His return], developing [that good work] *and* perfecting *and* bringing it to full completion in you.
> Philippians 1:6 Amplified

5. According to what God has promised, is there any reason for you not to have hope? Why or why not?

6. Spend some time thanking God for His promises to you.

Understanding the Good News - Lesson Two

Name_____Date_____

Answer the following questions. To turn in page to small group leader, use identical perforated page in back of book.

1. What has your understanding of salvation been before this lesson?

2. What new understanding of the "good news" did you gain from this lesson?

3. When did you personally believe the "good news" and receive eternal life?

4. Is there anything you have done that you believe God has not forgiven? If so, what?

5. How confident are you of God's presence in your daily life?

6. What wrong beliefs did you recognize from this week's lesson?

7. Mark the graph to indicate how much of this week's assignment you completed.

| None | 50% | 100% |

Record Your Prayer Requests:

Seeing Ourselves As God Sees Us - Day One

Goal: To understand what Scripture teaches about the nature of a child of God.

Before we can address our problem from God's perspective, we must first see ourselves from God's perspective.

It is important to realize that the dominant image of man in Scripture is as a whole being. That is, the terms *body, soul,* and *spirit* are frequently used interchangeably to mean "life." For example, Romans 12:1 teaches us to present our bodies to God.

> I urge you therefore, brethren, by the mercies of God, to present your bodies a living and holy sacrifice, acceptable to God, *which is* your spiritual service of worship.
>
> Romans 12:1 NAS

When we present our bodies to God, we present our whole life.

Although Scripture addresses us as whole beings, it uses the terms *body, soul* and *spirit,* also to teach us how we are to function within that whole.

> Now may the God of peace Himself sanctify you entirely; and may your spirit and soul and body be preserved complete, without blame at the coming of our Lord Jesus Christ.
>
> I Thessalonians 5:23 NAS

1. What do the following passages tell you about the human spirit?

> Then shall the dust [out of which God made man's body] return to the earth as it was, and the spirit shall return to God Who gave it.   Ecclesiastes 12:7 Amplified

> God is a Spirit (a spiritual Being) and those who worship Him must worship *Him* in spirit and in truth (reality).   John 4:24 Amplified

> The Spirit Himself [thus] testifies together with our own spirit, [assuring us] that we are children of God.   Romans 8:16 Amplified

Remembering that the body is our vehicle of performance or doing, our soul is our thinking, feeling and choosing, and our spirit is our life and identity.

2. List the characteristics of your old identity found in Ephesians 2:1-3; 4:17-22 as they relate to your body, soul, and spirit.

3. List the characteristics of your new identity in Christ found in Ezekiel 36:26-27, Romans 6:11, Romans 8:10, 16, Ephesians 4:24, Colossians 3:10-12, Galatians 5:22-23, and as they relate to your body, soul, and spirit.

Old Identity   New Identity

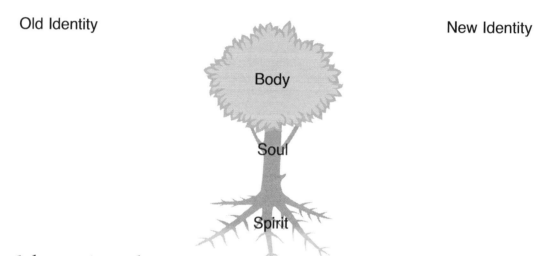

4. Read the article, "What Is Man", on page 3.23.

5. Based on what you have learned, what kind of nature do Christians have?

6. Write a thank-you note to God expressing gratefulness for His giving you a new spirit (nature).

Seeing Ourselves As God Sees Us - Day Two

Goal: To begin creating a Christian identity.

The following verses reveal that at salvation we were made into new beings. Although this is a reality, the understanding of our new nature must become ingrained into the very fabric of our identity. Remember that your spirit has been changed, but your soul is in the process of being renewed.

A new heart will I give you and a new spirit will I put within you, and I will take away the stony heart out of your flesh and give you a heart of flesh. And I will put My Spirit within you . . .
Ezekiel 36:26-27a Amplified

Therefore, if any man is in Christ, he is a new creature, the old things passed away; behold, new things have come.
2 Corinthians 5:17 NAS

Read "Becoming Who You Already Are" on page 3.27.

1. Select five statements from the first column on page 3.28 which reflect how you most often view yourself and write them below.	2. Now write out the corresponding truth from the second column and one of the verses given in the third column.	3. Write any thoughts or feelings you have which contradict this truth.

4. How do these negative thoughts affect your daily life?

   your behavior?

   your emotions?

   your relationships?

5. How do your negative thoughts and beliefs about yourself relate to your presenting problem from Week One - Day One?

6. The truest thing about you is what God says! These amazing truths must so permeate your thinking that they define how you see yourself so that you see life in light of who you are in Christ. Spend a few minutes thanking God for your salvation and for giving you a new spirit and a new identity.

Seeing Ourselves As God Sees Us - Day Three

Goal: To understand the person and role of the Holy Spirit in our lives.

1. The Holy Spirit is a person, not just a "power." Jesus calls Him, "the Spirit of Truth," "the Comforter," and "the Helper." After each verse below write the role of the Holy Spirit in the Christian's life.

> But the Comforter (Counselor, Helper, Intercessor, Advocate, Strengthener, Standby), the Holy Spirit, Whom the Father will send in My Name [in My place, to represent Me and act on My behalf], He will teach you all things. And He will cause you to recall (will remind you of, bring to your remembrance) everything I have told you.
>
> John 14:26 Amplified

> But when the Comforter (Counselor, Helper, Advocate, Intercessor, Strengthener, Standby) comes, Whom I will send to you from the Father, the Spirit of Truth Who comes (proceeds) from the Father, He [Himself] will testify regarding Me.
>
> John 15:26 Amplified

> But when He, the Spirit of Truth (the Truth-giving Spirit) comes, He will guide you into all the Truth (the whole, full Truth). For He will not speak His own message [on His own authority]; but He will tell whatever He hears [from the Father; He will give the message that has been given to Him], and He will announce *and* declare to you the things that are to come [that will happen in the future].
>
> John 16:13 Amplified

> Such hope never disappoints *or* deludes *or* shames us, for God's love has been poured out in our hearts through the Holy Spirit Who has been given to us.
>
> Romans 5:5 Amplified

So too the [Holy] Spirit comes to our aid *and* bears us up in our weakness; for we do not know what prayer to offer *nor* how to offer it worthily as we ought, but the Spirit Himself goes to meet our supplication *and* pleads in our behalf with unspeakable yearnings *and* groanings too deep for utterance.

Romans 8:26 Amplified

Now we have not received the spirit [that belongs to] the world, but the [Holy] Spirit Who is from God, [given to us] that we might realize *and* comprehend *and* appreciate the gifts [of divine favor and blessing so freely and lavishly] bestowed on us by God.

1 Corinthians 2:12 Amplified

But the fruit of the [Holy] Spirit [the work which His presence within accomplishes] is love, joy (gladness), peace, patience (an even temper, forbearance), kindness, goodness (benevolence), faithfulness, gentleness (meekness, humility), self-control (self-restraint, continence). Against such things there is no law [that can bring a charge].

Galatians 5:22-23 Amplified

2. Review your answers to question 1 and identify the areas for which you have been feeling responsible but which are actually the responsibility of the Holy Spirit.

3. The Holy Spirit is responsible for conforming us to Christ. Express your gratitude to God for the Holy Spirit's presence and ministry in your life. Admit to God the areas in which you have not acknowledged the Holy Spirit or depended on Him for your spiritual development.

Seeing Ourselves As God Sees Us - Day Four

Goal: To recognize that your part in experiencing your new identity is to live by faith.

The method of experiencing your new identity is to live by faith. Faith is taking God at His Word. Faith is our response to the revelation of Who God is and what He has done for us through Christ. Faith is a gift of God (Ephesians 2:8-9) which can increase over time, much like a muscle that grows stronger with use.

1. What does the following verse tell you regarding how we are saved?

> Because if you acknowledge *and* confess with your lips that Jesus is Lord and in your heart believe (adhere to, trust in, and rely on the truth) that God raised Him from the dead, you will be saved. For with the heart a person believes (adheres to, trusts in, and relies on Christ) and so is justified (declared righteous, acceptable to God), and with the mouth He confesses (declares openly and speaks out freely his faith) *and* confirms [his] salvation. Romans 10:9-10 Amplified

2. What does the following verse say regarding faith?

> So faith *comes* from hearing, and hearing by the Word of Christ. Romans 10:17, NAS

3. What does Colossians 2:6 say about how we are to walk (live moment by moment)?

> As you therefore have received Christ Jesus the Lord, so walk in Him. Colossians 2:6 NAS

4. According to Galatians 2:20, how are you to live?

> I have been crucified with Christ [in Him I have shared His crucifixion]; it is no longer I who live, but Christ (the Messiah) lives in me; and the life I now live in the body I live by faith in (by adherence to and reliance on and complete trust in) the Son of God, Who loved me and gave Himself up for me. Galatians 2:20 Amplified

5. Faith is not a feeling, nor is it intellectual knowledge. Who is to be the object of our faith, according to Hebrews 12:1-2?

> Therefore, since we have so great a cloud of witnesses surrounding us, let us also lay aside every encumbrance, and the sin which so easily entangles us, and let us run with endurance the race that is set before us, fixing our eyes on Jesus, the author and perfecter of faith, who for the joy set before Him endured the cross, despising the shame, and has sat down at the right hand of the throne of God.   Hebrews 12:1-2 NAS

We are not to put faith in our faith. Biblical faith is trust and reliance on the person and character of God. As you confess your new identity with your mouth and believe in your heart what God has said, the Holy Spirit will make it real in your experience (in God's time, not yours).

6. Spend a few minutes thanking God for your new identity (be specific), and express your trust in Him to make it your experience through the power of the Holy Spirit.

Seeing Ourselves As God Sees Us - Day Five

Goal: To understand how to experience your new identity, practically, in your daily life.

Experiencing your new identity is more than just a matter of replacing negative thoughts with more positive ones. It is the result of relating to God and believing what He says about who you are in Christ. Daily you choose to put off the old identity and put on your new identity.

1. Read the following passage several times.

> This I say therefore, and affirm together with the Lord, that you walk no longer just as the Gentiles also walk, in the futility of their mind,
>
> being darkened in their understanding, excluded from the life of God, because of the ignorance that is in them, because of the hardness of their heart;
>
> and they, having become callous, have given themselves over to sensuality, for the practice of every kind of impurity with greediness.
>
> But you did not learn Christ in this way, if indeed you have heard Him and have been taught in Him, just as truth is in Jesus,
>
> that, in reference to your former manner of life, you lay aside the old self (identity), which is being corrupted in accordance with the lusts of deceit,
>
> and that you be renewed in the spirit of your mind,
>
> and put on the new self, which in the likeness *of* God has been created in righteousness and holiness of the truth.   Ephesians 4:17-24 NAS

2. Ask the Holy Spirit to bring to your mind one area in your life where you are not presently experiencing your new identity in Christ.

3. Ask the Holy Spirit to show you the lies you are believing in this area of your life and the thoughts that need to be replaced with God's Truth. Write the lie that is to be put off and the truth that is to be put on.

4. For each lie you listed, write the truth about your new identity on a 3 x 5 card or post-it note, along with a corresponding verse of Scripture (refer to Day Two's handout, "Becoming Who You Already Are"). Now place these in prominent places (such as the bathroom mirror, refrigerator, dash of car, etc.) so you will be reminded of the truth throughout the day. When reminded of the truth, thank God (out loud if possible) for what is really true about you "in Christ." Continue this daily for the next three weeks.

Seeing Ourselves As God Sees Us - Lesson Three

Name _____ Date _____

Answer the following questions. To turn in page to small group leader, use identical perforated page in back of book.

1. According to what you have learned about the nature of man, what changed in you at salvation?

2. How does understanding that you have a new nature give you confidence concerning your salvation and spiritual growth?

3. What wrong beliefs about yourself do you need to put off?

4. How would believing your new identity and relying on the Holy Spirit in your daily life affect the way you respond to your present problems?

5. What questions do you have concerning the nature of man and your new identity?

6. Mark the graph to indicate how much of this week's assignment you completed.

None	50%	100%

3.21

Record Your Prayer Requests:

Getting to Know Our Heavenly Father - Day One

Goal: To recognize how your earthly father (or other authority figure) has influenced your emotional perception of God as your Heavenly Father.

1. Write a description of who your earthly father is to you.

2. Write who God the Father is to you (based on your emotional—**not** intellectual understanding of God).

3. Do you see any correlation between the way you view your earthly father and the way you view God as your Father? If so, in what ways?

4. Until we recognize the lies we're believing about God, we will probably not trust Him enough to turn to Him in a time of need or develop a close, intimate relationship with Him. Below are some common wrong perceptions we have about God.

    Evaluate your emotional perception of God (**not** what you know to be true) by circling the number that best describes your thoughts and feelings.

    0 = never 1 = seldom 2 = sometimes 3 = often 4 = usually 5 = always

Generally, in my relationship with God I feel:

Nothing (I don't feel His presence at all)	0	1	2	3	4	5
Abandoned (I have to do things myself)	0	1	2	3	4	5
Alone (I'm all by myself for solutions and strength)	0	1	2	3	4	5
Unsure (of what He thinks of me or where I stand with Him)	0	1	2	3	4	5
Uneasy (I don't know what to expect)	0	1	2	3	4	5

Generally I feel God is:

Inconsiderate (He doesn't take into account my feelings and forces me to do things I don't want to do or doesn't let me do things I want to do)	0	1	2	3	4	5
Hard to please (No matter what I do, it isn't good enough; or, I can't know what is expected from me; He's hard to please)	0	1	2	3	4	5
Conditionally loving (His love for me is based on my obedience)	0	1	2	3	4	5
Unloving (He sees my situation and allows me to suffer)	0	1	2	3	4	5
Angry/Judgmental (He is quick to punish me when I don't measure up; turns His back on me when I fail)	0	1	2	3	4	5

Impatient (He wants things done now!)	0	1	2	3	4	5
Critical (Most of what He thinks or says to me is negative)	0	1	2	3	4	5
Punishing (He's mad and withdraws or punishes me when I sin)	0	1	2	3	4	5
Hard to hear (I don't hear from Him, or I vaguely hear from Him)	0	1	2	3	4	5
Non-communicative (He doesn't talk to me much or at all)	0	1	2	3	4	5
Hard to understand (can't quite figure Him out—complicated)	0	1	2	3	4	5
Not helping me (I'm left to do it in my own strength)	0	1	2	3	4	5
Irresponsible (He's allowing all sorts of bad things to happen)	0	1	2	3	4	5
Slow (He takes His time changing me or getting things done)	0	1	2	3	4	5
Uncaring (He really doesn't care)	0	1	2	3	4	5
Tolerating my presence (He doesn't prefer me)	0	1	2	3	4	5

5. Now list the characteristics of God for which you circled 3 or higher on question 4.

6. What does the following verse tell you about your Heavenly Father?

> No man has ever seen God at any time; *the only unique Son, or* the only-begotten God, Who is in the bosom [in the intimate presence] of the Father, He has declared Him [He has revealed Him and brought Him out where He can be seen; He has interpreted Him and He has made Him known].
>
> John 1:18 Amplified

4.13

7. What does Jesus claim in the following verses?

> Jesus said to him, "I am the Way and the Truth and the Life; no one comes to the Father except by (through) Me.
>
> If you had known Me [had learned to recognize Me], you would also have known My Father. From now on, you know Him and have seen Him."
>
> Philip said to Him, "Lord, show us the Father [cause us to see the Father—that is all we ask]; then we shall be satisfied."
>
> Jesus replied, "Have I been with all of you for so long a time, and do you not recognize *and* know Me yet, Philip? Anyone who has seen Me has seen the Father. How can you say then, Show us the Father?
>
> Do you not believe that I am in the Father, and that the Father is in Me?"
>
> John 14:6-10a Amplified

8. According to these verses, how can we know what our Heavenly Father is like?

Getting to Know Our Heavenly Father - Day Two

Goal: To recognize and strengthen the areas where your concept of your Heavenly
Father is weak or distorted.

1. Relational Evaluation: This exercise allows you to evaluate your relationship with
   God as your Heavenly Father. Because it is subjective, there are no wrong answers.
   On a scale of 1-10, rate how real this characteristic is to you in your relationship with
   your Heavenly Father. Remember you are evaluating how much you experience this
   characteristic of God.

   Do you see your Heavenly Father as One who is:

Characteristic	Never . . . . Always
___ Loving	1 2 3 4 5 6 7 8 9 10
___ Caring	1 2 3 4 5 6 7 8 9 10
___ Forgiving	1 2 3 4 5 6 7 8 9 10
___ Compassionate	1 2 3 4 5 6 7 8 9 10
___ Giving	1 2 3 4 5 6 7 8 9 10
___ Understanding	1 2 3 4 5 6 7 8 9 10
___ Accepting	1 2 3 4 5 6 7 8 9 10
___ Satisfies	1 2 3 4 5 6 7 8 9 10
___ Persistently pursuing	1 2 3 4 5 6 7 8 9 10
___ Reasonable	1 2 3 4 5 6 7 8 9 10

2. Psalm 103 contains many characteristics of our Father-Savior. With each
   characteristic, provide the corresponding verse. Next, rate yourself as to how
   real this characteristic is to you in your relationship with God.

Characteristic	Verse	Never . . . . Always
___ Pardons	_____	1 2 3 4 5 6 7 8 9 10
___ Heals	_____	1 2 3 4 5 6 7 8 9 10
___ Redeems	_____	1 2 3 4 5 6 7 8 9 10
___ Lovingkindness	_____	1 2 3 4 5 6 7 8 9 10
___ Compassion	_____	1 2 3 4 5 6 7 8 9 10
___ Satisfies	_____	1 2 3 4 5 6 7 8 9 10
___ Renews	_____	1 2 3 4 5 6 7 8 9 10
___ Righteous	_____	1 2 3 4 5 6 7 8 9 10
___ Gracious	_____	1 2 3 4 5 6 7 8 9 10
___ Sovereign	_____	1 2 3 4 5 6 7 8 9 10

A rating of 1 to 6 probably indicates a wrong concept of God as Father-Savior. From this list and the list in question 5, Day One, identify the characteristics you need to experience more fully in your relationship with God and check them on the list below.

Loving — John 3:16; 1 Corinthians 13:4-8; 1 John 4:10
____ My Father-Savior loves me for who I am.
____ His love for me is unconditional and unceasing.

Caring — Matthew 6:26; 10:29-31; 1 Peter 5:7
____ My Father-Savior cares for me always.
____ His major concern is my well-being.

Forgiving — Psalm 103:12; Colossians 1:14; Hebrews 10:17
____ My Father-Savior has forgiven me unconditionally.
____ His forgiveness of my sins includes forgetfulness.

Compassionate — Exodus 33:19; Deuteronomy 4:31; Psalm 103:4-5
____ My Father-Savior is full of compassion toward me.
____ His compassion affirms me and supports me.

Giving — Psalm 37:4; Romans 8:32; James 1:17
____ My Father-Savior gives me the desires of my heart.
____ His giving nature withholds no good thing from me.

Understanding — Job 12:13; Psalm 139:1-2; Isaiah 40:28
____ My Father-Savior understands my thoughts and my actions.
____ His understanding of me gives me strength and comfort.

Accepting — Psalm 139:1-6; Romans 15:7
____ My Father-Savior accepts me totally and unconditionally.
____ His acceptance of me is based on who I am and not on what I do.

Satisfies — Psalm 107:9; Matthew 6:33; John 14:14; Ephesians 3:19
____ My Father-Savior fulfills my every need.
____ His grace provides a canopy of satisfaction for me.

Persistently pursuing — Luke 19:10; 1 Timothy 1:15; 2:4; Titus 2:11
____ My Father-Savior is the Hound of Heaven.
____ He moved Heaven and earth to bring me to Him.

Reasonable — Proverbs 3:5-6; Isaiah 1:18; Ephesians 3:12
____ My Father-Savior is completely approachable.
____ His attitude toward me is one of favor and good will.

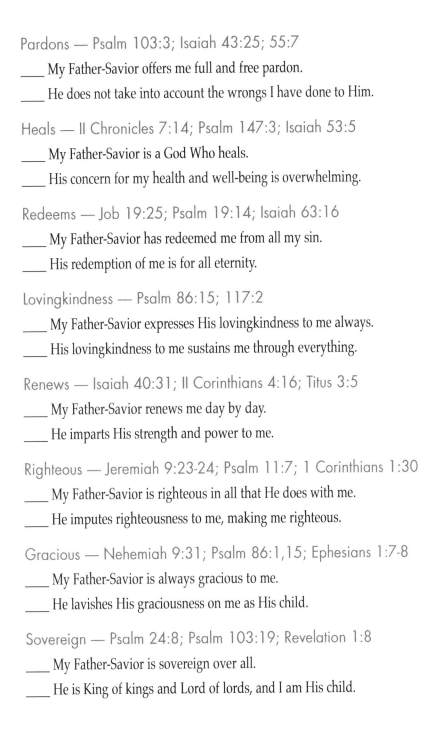

Pardons — Psalm 103:3; Isaiah 43:25; 55:7

____ My Father-Savior offers me full and free pardon.

____ He does not take into account the wrongs I have done to Him.

Heals — II Chronicles 7:14; Psalm 147:3; Isaiah 53:5

____ My Father-Savior is a God Who heals.

____ His concern for my health and well-being is overwhelming.

Redeems — Job 19:25; Psalm 19:14; Isaiah 63:16

____ My Father-Savior has redeemed me from all my sin.

____ His redemption of me is for all eternity.

Lovingkindness — Psalm 86:15; 117:2

____ My Father-Savior expresses His lovingkindness to me always.

____ His lovingkindness to me sustains me through everything.

Renews — Isaiah 40:31; II Corinthians 4:16; Titus 3:5

____ My Father-Savior renews me day by day.

____ He imparts His strength and power to me.

Righteous — Jeremiah 9:23-24; Psalm 11:7; 1 Corinthians 1:30

____ My Father-Savior is righteous in all that He does with me.

____ He imputes righteousness to me, making me righteous.

Gracious — Nehemiah 9:31; Psalm 86:1,15; Ephesians 1:7-8

____ My Father-Savior is always gracious to me.

____ He lavishes His graciousness on me as His child.

Sovereign — Psalm 24:8; Psalm 103:19; Revelation 1:8

____ My Father-Savior is sovereign over all.

____ He is King of kings and Lord of lords, and I am His child.

Now that you know the characteristics which need to be strengthened in your understanding of God, select one verse for each of those characteristics. Begin renewing your mind about Who your Father is by meditating each day on these verses. Spend some time now writing what your wrong thoughts have been and then write the right thoughts. Spend time talking to God and making a conscious choice to put off the wrong thoughts.

4.17

Wrong Thoughts about God
Put Off

Example:
I don't see how God could possibly love me.

Right Thoughts about God
Put On

Example:
My Father's love is unconditional and unchanging. It is not based on who I am, but Who He is.

Getting to Know Our Heavenly Father - Day Three

Goal: To know the character and heart of God the Father through His Son, Jesus Christ.

1. Describe how you view Jesus as a person.

2. What do the following verses tell you about Jesus?

> I and the Father are One. John 10:30 Amplified

> [Now] He is the exact likeness of the unseen God [the visible representation of the invisible]; He is the Firstborn of all creation. Colossians 1:15 Amplified

> For in Him the whole fullness of Deity (the Godhead) continues to dwell in bodily form [giving complete expression of the divine nature]. Colossians 2:9 Amplified

3. Compare your view of Jesus with your view of God the Father from Day One. What are the similarities and/or differences?

Often our view of Jesus is very different from our view of God the Father. This may be because we have developed our view of Jesus more from the stories in the Gospels, but we have based our view of God the Father more on our past experiences.

4. Read the following Scriptures and write how each verse describes Jesus.

Luke 19:10 _____

Matthew 9:10-13 _____

Matthew 9:36 _____

Matthew 11:28-30 _____

Matthew 23:37 _____

John 8:1-11 _____

John 10:11 _____

5. Seeing the Father through Jesus and learning to relate to Him in a personal and intimate way is vital. Spend a few minutes thanking God for Who He is and what He is really like. Ask God to reveal Himself to you more clearly and enable you to have a deeper, more intimate relationship with Him as your Father. Remember that His ability and desire to reveal Himself to you is greater than your ability and desire to see Him differently.

6. Continue to meditate on verses pertaining to God's character from Day Two.

Getting to Know Our Heavenly Father - Day Four

Goal: To begin recognizing and receiving your Heavenly Father's thoughts towards you.

> Many, O Lord my God, are the wonderful works which You have done, and Your thoughts toward us; no one can compare with You! If I should declare and speak of them, they are too many to be numbered.   Psalm 40:5 Amplified
>
> How precious *and* weighty also are Your thoughts to me, O God! How vast is the sum of them! If I could count them, they would be more in number than the sand.
> Psalm 139:17-18a Amplified

1. Read out loud the paraphrased, personalized verses on the next page, placing your name in the blanks.

2. Meditate on one of these verses during the next few days. Receive this as your Heavenly Father's thoughts toward you each morning before you start your day and each night before you go to sleep.

MY HEAVENLY FATHER'S THOUGHTS TOWARD ME

For I AM the Lord! Your Lord, _____, I AM merciful and gracious; slow to become angry and overflowing with lovingkindness and truth, maintaining lovingkindness toward you. I have forgiven your wickedness, rebellion and sin.   Exodus 34:6

For the Spirit which you received (at the moment of new birth) is not a spirit of slavery to return you to bondage to fear; rather you have received from Me the Spirit of adoption! I have made you My child and in the bliss and security of that position, _____, you can cry "Abba" or "Father" (Daddy)! The Holy Spirit Himself witnesses to your spirit telling you this is so, assuring you that you are My child.   Romans 8:15-16

_____, My child, do not dread, neither be afraid, for I AM the Lord your God (your Father) Who goes before you in your trouble; I will fight for you, just as I did the nation of Israel when I brought them out of Egypt. I will carry you just like I did them, just as a man carries his son.   Deuteronomy 1:29-31

This is what I, the Lord Who created you, Who formed you says; Fear not, _____, for I have redeemed you. I have bought you back for Myself by paying the price of My life instead of leaving you captive. I have called you personally by name, and you are Mine. Therefore, when you walk through the waters of trouble, I, your Father, will be with you, and as you go through the rivers, they will not overwhelm you; when you walk through the fire you shall not be burned or scorched, nor shall the flame touch you. Fear not because I, your Father, am with you. You are precious in My sight, and honored, and I love you!   Isaiah 43:1-4

Listen to Me, _____, I the Lord, your Father, have borne you from your birth; I carried you from the womb. Even to your old age I will remain the same, for I AM the source of supply for your every need; even until your hair is white with age, I, your Father will carry you, _____, and deliver you! Isaiah 46:3-4

And the Lord, your Father, declares to you: Can a woman forget her nursing child and have no compassion on the son of her womb? Yes, she may forget, yet your Father will not forget you, _____. See, I have indelibly tattooed a picture of you on the palm of each of My hands.   Isaiah 49:15-16

I, the Lord, your Father, have loved you, _____, with a love that never ends; therefore, with My favor and merciful kindness I have taken the initiative and have drawn you to myself.   Jeremiah 31:3

Fear not, _____, and don't let your hands sink down and don't be discouraged, for I AM with you in everything! I AM the Mighty One, the Savior Who saves! I AM rejoicing over you with joy! I rest in the silent satisfaction of your being My child and in the love that I have for you. I will never make mention of your past sins or even recall them. I delight in you and rejoice over you with singing!   Zephaniah 3:16-17

Dear Child, I made you alive when you were dead in your sins; those sins in which you, at one time, walked habitually. You were then destined for my wrath like the rest of mankind. But I, being rich in mercy and in order to satisfy the great and wonderful and intense love that I have for you, made you alive together in fellowship and in union with My Son Jesus, by giving you His very life. All because of My grace and mercy, which you did not deserve, you have been delivered from My righteous judgment. Not only have I made you alive to Me, _____, but I have raised you up with Jesus and have seated you with Him in the heavenly sphere, by virtue of your being IN Christ Jesus. I did this for you to demonstrate clearly for all eternity the immeasurable, limitless, surpassing riches of My free grace, given to you out of the kindness and goodness of My heart. For it is by My free and gracious love that you have been delivered from judgment and made a partaker of My salvation in Christ, which you have received by faith. Always remember your salvation is not of your own doing; you did not obtain it by your own striving or performance, but it is a free gift from Me, your Heavenly Father.   Ephesians 2:4-10

Getting to Know Our Heavenly Father - Day Five

Goal: To understand how to live and walk as God's child.

1. Read the article, "FatherCare" on page 4.27. Underline the important sentences that speak to you. Write out the main idea or thought you received from this article.

2. Ask God to reveal to you who/what you have turned to to meet your deepest need. Fill in the blanks below.

   I have primarily depended upon _____ to meet my need for love.

   I have tried to _____ in order to feel like I belong.

   I have depended on _____ to give me a sense of well-being.

   I have depended upon _____ to make me feel secure.

   I have looked to _____ for approval.

   I have tried to gain acceptance from _____ by _____.

   I have worshiped (valued) _____ more than God.

3. Pray the following prayer out loud to God.

Dear Heavenly Father, I have come to realize that I do not know You as You really are, and because of this, I have not experienced the kind of intimacy that You desire to have with me. I have looked to myself, others, and things to meet my deepest needs. I now desire for You to meet these needs by interacting with You daily in a close and intimate way. I want to know You as fully as possible, but I don't know how to get to know You. So, Father, I'm asking You to reveal Yourself to me through Your Word and in my daily life. Open my eyes that I might see Your glory, majesty, and goodness. Open my mind and heart to understand and to receive Your perfect unconditional love for me.

Getting to Know Our Heavenly Father - Lesson Four

Name _____ Date _____

1. What corrupted beliefs about God as Father did you recognize through this lesson?

2. How would knowing and relating to God as your Father affect your life (emotionally, relationally, behaviorally)?

3. How would relating to God as an unconditionally loving and perfect Father affect your life?

4. What from this week's assignment was most meaningful to you?

5. What characteristic(s) of God need strengthening in your life?

6. Mark the graph to indicate how much of this week's assignment you completed.

| None | 50% | 100% |

Record Your Prayer Requests:

Living By the Spirit - Day One

Goal: To understand the person of the Holy Spirit.

The Holy Spirit is God within us. He is more than a "power." He is a person Who has a mind (knows and communicates God's thoughts), a will (distributes gifts as He wills—1 Corinthians 12:11), and emotions (can be grieved, made sorrowful—Ephesians 4:30). He is called the "Spirit of Truth" in John 15:26.

1. In John 14:26, what is the Holy Spirit called?

2. In John 15:26, what is the Holy Spirit called?

3. Who is sending Him?

4. In Romans 8:2, what is the Holy Spirit called?

5. How does Isaiah 11:2 describe the Holy Spirit?

6. Galatians 5:22-23 lists some of the fruit of the Spirit. What emotions does this list indicate that the Holy Spirit has?

7. Write each of the nine characteristics of the fruit of the Spirit out in this manner:

   1) The Holy Spirit is love.

   2)

   3)

   4)

   5)

   6)

   7)

   8)

   9)

8. Based on what you've just read about the Holy Spirit, write your own description of Who the Holy Spirit is to you personally.

9. Is this the type of person you could trust? Why or why not?

10. According to 1 Corinthians 6:19, what is your body?

11. According to Romans 12:1, what are you to do?

12. Spend a few minutes expressing to God your desire for the Holy Spirit to live through you. Pray Romans 12:1 back to God, offering your body (life) to Him.

Living By the Spirit - Day Two

Goal: To understand the Holy Spirit's role in your life.

1. What does John 6:63 tell us the Spirit does?

2. According to John 14:17, where does the Holy Spirit live?

3. Read the following verses and write what the Holy Spirit will do for you.

    a) John 14:26

    b) John 16:13

    c) Romans 5:5

    d) Romans 8:15

    e) Romans 8:16

    f) Romans 8:27

    g) Romans 15:13

4. Read John 15:1-5. The word "abide" means to dwell or make yourself at home. Abiding in Jesus is simply giving oneself to Him to be ruled and taught and led, thereby resting in His unconditional love. According to verse 4 and 5, how much of the Christian life can you accomplish on your own?

5. In what ways have you tried to live the Christian life on your own?

6. Write down some personal examples of how the Holy Spirit has been working in your life until now (reflect on your answers to question 3).

7. Write a thank-you note to the Holy Spirit, expressing your gratitude for all He has already done for you.

Living By the Spirit - Day Three

Goal: To recognize your need to walk by faith and depend moment-by-moment on the Holy Spirit.

Jesus described the Spirit-filled life as thirsting and drinking and walking. Each of these activities is repetitive in nature.

> If we live by the Spirit, let us also walk by the Spirit.   Galatians 5:25 NAS

> As you have therefore received Christ . . . so walk in Him. Colossians 2:6 NAS

1. How did you receive Christ? How are you to walk?

2. We exercise faith in Christ not only at salvation but also daily, moment-by-moment. With each new situation or need, we need to express faith in Christ, Who is our life. Read Galatians 2:20. How does Paul say he now lives?

3. Read John 7:37-39. Thirst expresses our continuous need and desire to know God. How often during a day do you get thirsty? How often do you think of trusting Jesus?

4. The following verses express the psalmist's longing for God. Write your own psalm expressing your thirst to God.

> As the deer pants for the water brooks,
> So my soul longs for Thee, O God.
> My soul thirsts for God, for the living God.
>   Psalm 42:1-2a, NAS

5. Drinking expresses receiving by faith. Every time we are thirsty (long for God) we acknowledge His presence (by talking to Him). Then, by trusting in Jesus, our soul is filled with His life-giving Spirit.

> If any man is thirsty, let him come to Me and drink. He who believes in Me, as the Scripture said, 'From his innermost being shall flow rivers of living water.'
>
> John 7:37b-38 NAS

6. Read John 4:5-24 about Jesus and the Samaritan woman. How was the woman trying to satisfy her thirst (her inward needs)? What did Jesus offer her?

7. Read John 5:38-40. Jesus was addressing the religious leaders who knew the Scriptures well. In fact, they had memorized most of it. What were these religious people missing? Why?

8. How have you tried to satisfy your thirst? (relationships, approval of others, material possessions, job, fame, etc.)

9. Write Galatians 2:20, personalizing it and putting it into your own words.

10. Express to Jesus your desire to trust Him moment by moment to satisfy your deepest needs and desires.

Living By the Spirit - Day Four

Goal: To understand the negative consequences of choosing to live according to the flesh and the value of living by the Spirit.

Living by the flesh is simply living by our own natural abilities, energy, and strength to meet our needs apart from God. Although the flesh might even appear very good and respectable, it can never produce God's quality of life.

After God promised Sarah and Abraham a son, Sarah persuaded Abraham to father a child by her handmaid, Hagar. This produced Ishmael, who persecuted Isaac, the son promised by God. These two sons represent the difference between living by the flesh and living by the Spirit.

1. Read Galatians 4:22-24; 28-29. Ishmael represents depending on our own energy, natural ability and strength. Isaac, the son of promise, represents the supernatural life of the Spirit. In what ways have you tried to fulfill God's plan for your life through your own energy, natural ability, and strength?

2. Through the life of the Apostle Peter, we can see the contrast between the flesh and the Spirit. Before the Holy Spirit was given, Peter was earnest in his efforts to follow Christ, but all his human effort ended in his denying Christ. Read Matthew 26:26, 31-35.

3. After the Holy Spirit was given on the day of Pentecost, Peter courageously and boldly proclaimed the Gospel. Even when experiencing physical suffering and persecution, Peter rejoiced in the Lord and continued to proclaim Him to others. Read Acts 4:13; 5:27-29.

4. Read Philippians 3:3-6. Describe the Apostle Paul's flesh.

5. Read John 6:63. What did Jesus say about the Spirit and the flesh?

6. Read 1 Corinthians 2:7-13. What does the Spirit reveal to your mind?

7. Looking back over today's answers, what personal benefit do you think you would receive by being motivated, led, and empowered by the Holy Spirit?

8. How would living by the Spirit change you in the midst of your present struggles and how you view your present circumstances?

9. In what areas do you need to receive God's wisdom?

10. In what areas do you need to receive God's strength?

11. In what ways do you need to be comforted by God?

12. Spend some time thanking God for being your resident Counselor, Teacher, Comforter, Helper, and Strengthener. Ask Him to remind you of how He has been all of these to you in the past. Ask Him to make you more aware of His presence in the future.

Living By the Spirit - Day Five

Goal: To recognize and correct any wrong beliefs that hinder you from experiencing a Spirit-filled life.

Living life by the Spirit requires living by faith (taking God at His Word). It means believing that the Holy Spirit indwells you and desires to live through your soul and body (Romans 8:15; 1 Corinthians 3:16).

Christ is the only Person capable of living the Christian life! No matter how sincere and determined our self-efforts are, we fail to love God and others as God has instructed us. However, the Holy Spirit fulfills God's righteous requirements by filling our souls with Christ's life. By faith, we accept that, in Christ, God has fulfilled all His righteous requirements for holiness and that Christ now lives in us and is our life.

In faith, we ask the Spirit to fill us (Ephesians 5:18), trusting Him to give us the power to live an abundant and Godly life. In faith, we accept that God has given us new hearts that desire to please Him, has poured out His love into our hearts, and has written His commandments on our hearts (Ezekiel 36:26-27; Romans 5:5).

1. According to the following verse, what is God's will concerning how you are to walk?

> Therefore be careful how you walk, not as unwise men, but as wise, making the most of your time, because the days are evil. So then do not be foolish, but understand what the will of the Lord is. And do not get drunk with wine, for that is dissipation, but be [continually] filled with the Spirit.   Ephesians 5:15-18, NAS

To be filled with the Spirit means to be stimulated, empowered, and influenced by the Holy Spirit who lives in you. To be filled, we must surrender control of our lives to the Holy Spirit (Romans 12:1) and allow Him to live through us. This is not a one-time experience but a day-to-day, moment-by-moment lifestyle.

2. Read Ephesians 5:15-18 again.

We are filled with the Holy Spirit by faith. Christ lives through you by the power of His Holy Spirit.

3. Read Galatians 2:20. Ask Him to begin teaching you how to live by faith in the Spirit.

4. Read the chart, "Common Wrong Beliefs About the Spirit-filled Life." Write out the wrong beliefs that best represent your thinking, then read the corresponding truth and Scriptures.

5. Choose to put off the lies you have believed about the Spirit, and replace them with the truth based on Scripture. Ask the Holy Spirit to remind you when the lies influence your thoughts again.

Being "filled" with the Holy Spirit is not a one-time experience, but a day-to-day, moment-by-moment lifestyle. To be filled, we must surrender control of our lives to the Holy Spirit.

6. Read the following verses, then take a few minutes to express to God your decision to yield control of your life to Him and to be filled with His Spirit.

> Or do you not know that your body is a temple of the Holy Spirit who is in you, whom you have from God, and that you are not your own? For you have been bought with a price: therefore glorify God in your body.　1 Corinthians 6:19-20 NAS

> But if the Spirit of Him who raised Jesus from the dead dwells in you, He who raised Christ Jesus from the dead will also give life to your mortal bodies through His Spirit who indwells you. So then, brethren, we are under obligation, not to the flesh, to live according to the flesh—for if you are living according to the flesh, you must die; but if by the Spirit you are putting to death the deeds of the body, you will live.　Romans 8:11-13 NAS

Living By the Spirit - Lesson Five

Name _____ Date _____

Answer the following questions. To turn in page to small group leader, use identical perforated page in back of book.

1. What encouraged you most about this week's study on the Holy Spirit?

2. List any fears or concerns you have about surrendering control of your life to the Holy Spirit.

3. What do you feel would keep God from filling you with His Spirit?

4. How would living by the Spirit affect your life and your current struggles?

5. Mark the graph to indicate how much of this week's assignment you completed.

None	50%	100%

Record Your Prayer Requests:

Controlling Emotions - Day One

Goal: To recognize how you deal with your negative emotions, and to begin to interact with God concerning them.

1. What emotions were expressed in your home as you were growing up?

   Which ones were "acceptable"? Which ones were "unacceptable"?

2. Presently, what emotions are you comfortable in expressing?

   Uncomfortable expressing?

   Comfortable with others expressing?

   Uncomfortable with others expressing?

3. What are your "red flags" that indicate you may be feeling an emotion but not acknowledging it? (Examples: yelling, physical stress, short temper, withdrawal, compulsive behavior such as overeating, etc.)

4. Review your answers from Week 1, Day 1. How were your problems affecting you emotionally?

5. Our emotions are messengers alerting us to something in our thoughts and beliefs. What are some thoughts and beliefs that your emotions may reveal?

6. When our emotions are more real to us than God's truth and we base our decisions and responses upon them, then our emotions are messy. Possible responses to these negative emotions include denying, "stuffing," venting on others, and expressing them to God. How have you handled these negative emotions in the past? (Example: When I feel depressed, I ignore it by eating or watching TV.)

7. How did these emotions affect your behavior and/or choices?

8. Take a few moments to interact with God. First, compare your, beliefs, thoughts, and behaviors with God's Word. Ask the Holy Spirit to reveal to you any inconsistencies, and confess (agree with God) those that He reveals. Then, decide how you need to change your thoughts, beliefs, and behavior to be consistent with God's truth. Next, ask the Holy Spirit to help change your behavior and to continue to reveal incorrect beliefs and thoughts. Remember, each time you experience a negative emotion or the Holy Spirit reveals a wrong belief or thought, you need to replace that belief or thought with God's truth.

Controlling Emotions - Day Two

Goal: To recognize the emotional side of God in Scripture.

1. Read the following verses, and list the emotions that God expresses.

    Genesis 6:5-6

    Psalm 145:8

    Psalm 149:4

    Isaiah 57:16

    Isaiah 62:5

    Mark 10:21

    Luke 13:34

    Luke 22:44

    John 11:33-36

    Hebrews 5:7

2. Compare and/or contrast these verses with how you have previously viewed God.

3. Read the following verses to learn how God feels about your emotions. Write how God feels about or responds to your emotions.

    Psalm 51:17

    Psalm 56:8

    Matthew 11:28

    John 20:24-28

    Hebrews 4:15-16

    1 Peter 5:7

4. Compare and/or contrast these verses with how you have previously thought that God feels about your emotions.

Controlling Emotions - Day Three

Goal: To see the Biblical pattern for managing your emotions.

1. The Biblical pattern for REED (what to do with emotions) is especially noticeable in Psalms 55 and 73.

> **R**ecognize your emotions.
>
> **E**xpress them to God (don't ignore them, stuff them or lash out toward others).
>
> **E**valuate (ask the Holy Spirit to show you) what your emotions and thoughts reveal about what you are believing.
>
> **D**ecide to agree with God about the truth (believe), and act in faith on that truth.

REED applies to both positive and negative emotions. However, all emotions are actually positive, because they help us turn to God and evaluate our thinking and beliefs.

2. Read Psalm 73 in the chronological order provided below and answer the questions.

RECOGNIZE: (verses 2-14) What emotions does the Psalmist experience?

EXPRESS: (verses 16, 21-22) How does the Psalmist express his emotions to God? List some of the statements he makes.

EVALUATE: (verses 17-20, 1, 23-27) What beliefs do his emotions reveal?

DECIDE: (verse 28) How does the Psalmist choose to act on the truth (rather than on his emotions)?

3. Ask the Holy Spirit to remind you to practice REED in your communication with God.

Controlling Emotions - Day Four

Goal: To begin using the REED method of managing your emotions.

1. Emotions, both pleasant and unpleasant, are a normal part of the Christian life. Think back to the last time you were struggling with negative emotions. Use the chart on page 6.23 to help you recognize your feelings and list them below.

2. Now express your feelings to God by writing the thoughts that prompted you to feel this way. Be as honest as possible. God already knows and accepts you. He never condemns or rejects you because of your emotional struggles.

3. Emotions are the result of thoughts and beliefs. Now, evaluate your thoughts by answering the following questions:
   A. What beliefs do your thoughts reveal about God, yourself, and your circumstances?

   B. What is the truth according to God's Word? (Refer to the "Father/God" Bible study, pages 4.15-4.18, and the "Creating a Christian Identity" sheet page 3.28 for the truth).

4. Next, decide to reject the lies you've been thinking and to replace them with the truth. Make a deliberate choice to walk by faith, accepting God's Word as your final authority. Ask God what steps of faith (action) He wants you to take.

5. For the rest of this week practice the REED method whenever you encounter negative or painful emotions. You may want to journal (write) your thoughts and feelings using the worksheet on pages 6.25 and 6.26.

Controlling Emotions - Day Five

Goal: To recognize and express your fears to God and learn to trust in Him when you are afraid.

One of our most painful emotions is fear—which is often disguised as worry, anger, or depression. It is one of the most difficult emotions to acknowledge. Often we've been taught that fear is a sign of weakness; therefore, we've learned to suppress it.

1. King David, a man after God's heart, often experienced fear. Read Psalm 56.

2. What did David fear? (see verses 2, 5-6)

3. What did David do when he was afraid? (see verses 1, 3-4, 9-13)

4. Think of a specific situation which causes you to be afraid. It might be a future event, or it may be the fear of failure or rejection. Use the REED method for taking this fear to God.

   RECOGNIZE: Ask God to help you identify what you are afraid of. Acknowledge your fear to yourself and God.

   EXPRESS: Write to God what you fear and why you are afraid.

EVALUATE: Consider what your thoughts and feelings tell you about your beliefs about this issue. What beliefs about God does your fear reveal? How does what you think and believe compare with God's Word?

DECIDE: Choose to agree with God's truth about this issue. Then, choose to act on that truth, knowing that the Holy Spirit will empower you.

Example: "Father, I am afraid my husband may lose his job. It's hard for me to trust You in this area when I think of our family's needs. Thank You for listening and caring about how I feel. I know You promise to meet all our needs (Philippians 4:19), so I am casting all my cares on You (1 Peter 5:7). Therefore, I choose to go about my day, not focusing on the potential problem, but trusting You to work this out for our good and to meet our needs in Your way and in Your timing."

Controlling Emotions - Lesson Six

Name _____ Date _____

Answer the following questions. To turn in page to small group leader, use identical perforated page in back of book.

1. What negative emotion did you experience most this past week? What kind of thoughts usually produced this emotion?

2. What did these thoughts tell you about what you were believing?

3. What new insight or perspective did God give you when you expressed your feelings honestly to Him?

4. How will practicing REED improve your relationship with God and your quality of life?

5. Mark the graph to indicate how much of this week's assignment you completed.

None	50%	100%

Record Your Prayer Requests:

Expectations, Anger, and Bitterness - Day One

Goal: To gain a Biblical perspective of anger and recognize the underlying cause of it.

When you acknowledge and take responsibility for your anger, victory over the anger becomes a distinct probability rather than a remote possibility. You may have "reason" for your anger, but do you have the "right" to stay angry? Have you reserved for yourself the "right" to be angry? No matter the reason for your anger, you must understand that you CHOOSE to stay angry.

1. To gain a Biblical perspective of anger, write out the main point of the following passages.

   Proverbs 29:11

   Proverbs 19:11

   Proverbs 29:22

   Ephesians 4:26-27

   Colossians 3:8-9

   James 1:19-20

2. List at least five expectations you have of yourself or others which, when not met, make you feel angry (irritated, frustrated, outraged, etc.). Circle the "+" if you think these expectations are presently being met, and circle the "-" if you think they are not being met.

   a) _____ + -

   b) _____ + -

   c) _____ + -

   d) _____ + -

   e) _____ + -

3. Everyone has needs. When our needs are not met, we often feel hurt or angry. Listed below are a number of needs that we have. Circle the "+" if you think the need is being met, and circle the "-" if you think the need is not being met. Circle the letter that corresponds with the person(s) you think should meet this need: (Y) Yourself, (S) Spouse, (P) Parent, (O) Others.

1)	To be loved	Y S P O	+ -
2)	To be needed	Y S P O	+ -
3)	To be understood	Y S P O	+ -
4)	To be wanted	Y S P O	+ -
5)	To be cared for	Y S P O	+ -
6)	To have significance	Y S P O	+ -
7)	To be approved of	Y S P O	+ -
8)	To be secure	Y S P O	+ -
9)	To belong	Y S P O	+ -
10)	To be fulfilled	Y S P O	+ -

4. One of the major causes of anger is thinking that our "rights" have been denied. Which of the "rights" listed below do you think of as being your personal "right"? Circle the "-" if the right is being denied, and list by whom the right is being denied.

By Whom

1)	To be treated fairly	-	_____
2)	To make my own decisions	-	_____
3)	To date	-	_____
4)	To have self-expression	-	_____
5)	To do my own thing	-	_____
6)	To be obeyed	-	_____
7)	To have my own money	-	_____
8)	To have privacy	-	_____
9)	To my own opinion	-	_____
10)	To have my own friends	-	_____
11)	To be protected	-	_____
12)	To be free	-	_____
13)	To be appreciated	-	_____
14)	To be heard	-	_____
15)	To receive affection	-	_____

5. Read Philippians 2:5-11. What rights do you think Jesus surrendered? Are you willing to yield your rights and trust God to meet your needs and exalt you in His way and in His time? As you pray about this, ask God to empower you to surrender all of your rights to Him.

Expectations, Anger, and Bitterness - Day Two

Goal: To learn to prevent and deal with anger by recognizing and yielding
expectations to God.

When an expectation is blocked or unmet, often our immediate emotional response is anger. Ephesians 4:26-27 tells us to, "be angry, and yet do not sin; do not let the sun go down on your anger, and do not give the devil an opportunity (foothold)." Unresolved anger leads to bitterness, and bitterness to resentment, vengeance, ingratitude, and depression.

1. Read over the "Expectations, Anger, and Bitterness" worksheet on page 7.21. Describe a situation that causes you continual anger.

2. What expectations are unmet? If you don't know, refer to Day One answers.

3. Choose to yield your expectations to God, and trust Him to meet your need in whatever way HE sees best. How would this change your response to the situation or person?

Anger as an emotion is not sinful. The wrong beliefs, attitudes, and actions which follow are what are sinful and need to be changed.

> And do not grieve the Holy Spirit of God, by whom you were sealed for the day of redemption. Let all bitterness and wrath and anger and clamor and slander be put away from you, along with all malice. And be kind to one another, tender-hearted, forgiving each other, just as God in Christ also has forgiven you.
>
> Ephesians 4:30-32 NAS

4. What beliefs, attitudes, or actions do you need to change? Whom do you need to forgive?

5. Write a prayer asking God to enable you to forgive and to accept those who are not fulfilling your expectations.

Expectations, Anger, and Bitterness - Day Three

Goal: To understand God's forgiveness of you and to recognize obstacles to forgiving others.

1. Often we have misconceptions about what forgiveness really involves. Read the list of "Common Misconceptions Regarding Forgiveness" on page 7.22, and check those that you have used to define forgiveness in the past.

2. Forgiving others is difficult until we have received God's total forgiveness for ourselves. Is there anything that you have done that still causes you to feel shame or guilt?

3. Read Matthew 18:21-35. Jesus taught this parable to demonstrate four important aspects of forgiveness:

   1) Forgiveness is a gift we do not deserve.
   2) It is erasing or foregoing what we feel is due us, canceling the debt owed, and yielding our rights and expectations.
   3) Once received from God, it is to be given to others.
   4) Unforgiveness results in personal torture and inner torment.

4. In Christ there is complete forgiveness.

> And when you were dead in your transgressions and the uncircumcision of your flesh, He made you alive together with Him, having forgiven us ALL our transgressions, having canceled out the certificate of debt consisting of decrees against us *and* which was hostile to us; and He has taken it out of the way, and nailed it to the cross.
> Colossians 2:13-14, NAS (emphasis added)

In the Roman courts of law, when a person was charged with a crime, a "certificate of debt" was written against him. This indictment stated the charge or charges against the person, and a due penalty was demanded. If the person charged was found guilty, he was removed to prison. The "certificate of debt" was nailed to his prison door. Once he had completed his sentence he was freed, and the words "paid in full" were stamped on the certificate of debt. The last words of Jesus on the cross were "It is finished." Incredibly, the word "finished" is the same word that was stamped on the certificate of debt, "paid in full"! Jesus paid in full the penalty for all our sins.

> By this will we have been sanctified through the offering of the body of Jesus Christ once for all. And every priest stands daily ministering and offering time after time the same sacrifices, which can never take away sins; but He, having offered one sacrifice for sins for all time, SAT DOWN AT THE RIGHT HAND OF GOD, . . . For by one offering He has perfected for all time those who are sanctified. "AND THEIR SINS AND THEIR LAWLESS DEEDS I WILL REMEMBER NO MORE." Now where there is forgiveness of these things, there is no longer *any* offering for sin. Since, therefore, brethren, we have confidence to enter the holy place by the blood of Jesus.
> Hebrews 10:10-12, 14, 17-19 NAS (emphasis added)

Is there any sin that Jesus hasn't forgiven? What?

5. It is essential and imperative that you accept what God says and receive His total and complete forgiveness. Verbalize your gratitude to Him (be specific).

Expectations, Anger, and Bitterness - Day Four

Goal: To begin resolving any unforgiveness and bitterness in your life.

Forgiveness is a decision, a choice based on an act of the will, not a feeling. It is a rational choice I make because I have been totally and completely forgiven by God. I have been made a forgiving person by nature in Christ. Therefore, not to forgive is to act contrary to my identity in Christ. Therefore, forgiveness includes:

a. Acknowledging the hurt.

b. Acknowledging how I felt.

c. Releasing the person from the debt owed me. (Saying in effect: "You never have to make it up to me or repay me. You are now free. You are forgiven. I release you...the debt is canceled.")

d. Accepting the person unconditionally, just as he is, and letting God change him. It requires releasing the person from the responsibility to love and accept me. I look to Christ alone to meet my need for security and significance and yield the right to judge the other person.

e. Being willing to risk being hurt again in the future should God allow it. In other words, I take down my wall of self-protection and trust Christ as my Wisdom and Protection should I get hurt again.

1. Some reasons why we fail to forgive are listed on page 7.23. Circle the number of each one that applies to you.

2. Describe an incident in your past that causes ongoing hurt.

3. On a separate piece of paper list each person who has contributed to your hurt, specifically stating the offense and the resulting emotions. The following outline may be helpful.

    1) "God, it hurt me when . . . " (Be specific).

    2) "And I felt . . . "

    3) "I now choose to forgive _____ . "

    4) "I accept _____ unconditionally, which means my love and acceptance of _____ does not depend on _____ or _____ performance now or in the future. I accept _____ just the way _____ is . . . even if _____ never changes...even if _____ gets worse."

    5) "I release _____ from the responsibility to meet my needs for love and acceptance. I choose to trust Jesus alone as the only one who can truly meet all my needs."

    6) "I am willing to risk being hurt again by _____ and trust Jesus as my Wisdom and Protection in the future about _____ and this matter."

    7) "God, I give You permission to change or to not change my feelings, according to Your time schedule."

Remember, forgiveness is primarily for your benefit. Revealing to the offender that you have forgiven _____ is not necessary or desirable unless he requests your forgiveness.

4. Now after you have walked through the steps of forgiveness, destroy this list.

Expectations, Anger, and Bitterness - Day Five

Goal: To recognize and remove a root of bitterness.

Bitterness is to the soul what cholesterol is to the arteries. Bitterness blocks the flow of the living water, limiting our capacity to be filled with the Holy Spirit.

> And do not grieve the Holy Spirit of God, by whom you were sealed for the day of redemption. Let all bitterness and wrath and anger and clamor and slander be put away from you, along with all malice.   Ephesians 4:30-31 NAS

> Pursue peace with all men . . . See to it that no one comes short of the grace of God; that no root of bitterness springing up causes trouble, and by it many be defiled.
>   Hebrews 12:14a, 15 NAS

The root of bitterness is invisible, but it produces visible fruit such as:

- Withdrawal from God
- Inability to love others
- Spiritual doubt and unbelief
- Depression
- Physical problems

The solution for bitterness is forgiveness. Cleansing our hearts of bitterness is often a long process when there has been an accumulation of unresolved anger and hurt. The following exercise may take some extra time to complete. No matter how long it takes, it will be worth it. Gaining freedom from bitterness will bring new freedom and joy in your life.

1. Ask the Holy Spirit to bring to your mind each event in your past that still stands out as an unpleasant or painful experience. Make a list on a separate piece of paper, writing down just a few words to identify the incident.

2. Below each incident list each person who contributed to your hurt.

3. List each wrong you suffered from each person.

4. Review the handout, "Reasons Why We Don't Forgive" on page 7.23. Note which ones apply in each situation.

Remember, forgiveness is primarily for your benefit. Now it is your nature to forgive as God has forgiven you.

5. One by one, verbalize to God your decision to forgive each person. Yield your "right" to punish the person in any way. Trust God to deal with each one as He sees best (Romans 12:19). *

6. Thank God for His faithfulness to use even the most hurtful incidents in your life for your ultimate good (Genesis 50:20; 1 Thessalonians 5:18; Romans 8:28).

7. Ask God to help you see each person who has hurt you the way He does and to empower you to love each one unconditionally (Matthew 5:43-48; Luke 6:27-38).

8. When you have completed this exercise, write "Paid In Full" across your list, and destroy it.

* If you still find this too painful or difficult, you may need a trusted friend, pastor, or Biblical personal guidance minister to pray with you.

Expectations, Anger, and Bitterness - Lesson Seven

Name _____ Date _____

Answer the following questions. To turn in page to small group leader, use identical perforated page in back of book.

1. About what have you been the most angry?

2. What expectations or rights are you holding onto that are contributing to this anger?

3. How are unforgiveness and bitterness affecting your life and relationships?

4. Have you forgiven those who have hurt you? If not, what do you think are the obstacles to forgiving them?

5. Whom did God lead you to forgive through this assignment?

6. Mark the graph to indicate how much of this week's assignment you completed.

None	50%	100%

Record Your Prayer Requests:

Expectations, Anger, and Bitterness Worksheet

Expectations	Anger	Bitterness				
Needs	Prevention:	Cure:	Resentment			
Comparisons	Yield expectations as act of trust in God.	Forgiveness		Vengeance		
Verbal Commitments					Ingratitude	
						Depression

Throughout life, we all develop expectations. They are usually produced by comparing ourselves with others ("They get to, so why can't I?") or from commitments people make or imply. Some expectations result from valid needs in our lives, such as being loved, accepted, and feeling secure. When those expectations are not met in the ways we want them to be met by others or by God, the emotional reaction is often anger.

The Bible says to "be angry, and yet do not sin" (Ephesians 4:26). Anger becomes a problem when we deal with it improperly. A way to safeguard against responding in anger is to yield our expectations to God. In yielding, I choose to let God meet my needs in the ways He sees best, not in the ways in which I want to see things done. I decide to trust Him and look to Him as the source of my contentment, joy, and security, instead of looking to circumstances or to other people.

However, what if I don't recognize an expectation I have and I get angry? What if the anger remains in my heart and turns into bitterness? To deal with anger and bitterness, I can choose to forgive others for what has happened and release them from my expectations. God will deal with them, so I defer that right to Him. If I do not deal with the bitterness, its roots grow down deeper and deeper into resentment, vengeance, and depression (Hebrews 12:15). I become unable to be satisfied and focus totally on the unmet expectation and the one who failed to meet it. I become unable to see how God is meeting my needs. But, what if the anger is at God? Then, I must make a choice to trust in God's loving and merciful character, that He is working all circumstances in my life for the good (Romans 8:28) and that He will provide my every need (Philippians 4:19) in His way.

ASSIGNMENT:

1. List any incident in your past that causes ongoing hurt. List each person who has contributed to your hurts.

2. Ask God to make you willing to forgive these people, and even yourself, and to trust Him to work all together for good.

3. By faith, choose to forgive the offenders by an act of your will, apart from what your emotions or reason are telling you. Verbalize this choice to God. Trust God to change your feelings of anger and hurt in His timing.

COMMON MISCONCEPTIONS REGARDING FORGIVENESS

I feel like I have forgiven _____ because:

_____ I don't feel angry anymore. Forgiveness is not feeling angry anymore.

_____ I am able to justify, understand, and explain away this person's hurtful behavior. I can see some of the reasons why he did it.

_____ I am able to put myself in his shoes and see things from his point of view.

_____ I am able to separate the person from their behavior. Forgiveness is being able to say, "What a person does and who he is, are two different things."

_____ I am giving him the benefit of the doubt. He didn't mean it. Forgiveness says no one is perfect, so you need to cut people some slack.

_____ I am saying to myself "time heals all wounds." I am willing to be patient and go on with my life. Forgiveness is a process that takes a lot of time.

_____ I am willing just to forget about it. Forgiving is forgetting...it is saying, "Let's just forget about it."

_____ I am able to pray for the person who has hurt me. I have asked God to forgive him.

_____ I am waiting for him to come to me and ask for my forgiveness. Once he does this, I will forgive him. I am willing to forgive.

_____ I have confronted this person about his behavior.

_____ I am able to say that I haven't really been hurt that badly. I just pretend that the hurt was really not that big of a thing.

_____ I am able to act as if it never happened.

_____ I have attempted reconciliation. Forgiveness says that the broken relationship must be restored.

_____ I am willing to go to the person and tell him that I forgive him.

_____ I am willing to be nice, take him a gift, and "turn the other cheek."

_____ I am trying to behave in a forgiving manner.

_____ I am trying to pretend that everything is OK and go on with my life and not bring the matter up again.

In short, forgiveness is none of the above items. Some of these may help in the process of getting ready to forgive, or they may be products of the forgiveness process, but they are not actually the same as forgiveness.

Reasons I Don't Forgive

1. Pride: forgiving someone makes me look weak. I want to be strong and superior. I'm right and I don't have to give in. *But pride is what keeps me in bondage and hinders growth.*

2. I don't want to give up my excuse-making system. *At first, freedom can be scary. I am out of my comfort zone. I will be learning a whole new way of living if I learn to forgive.*

3. If I were to forgive I would feel out of control. I want to feel in control and be able to manipulate others by holding the debt against them. *The truth is I am out of control when I cling to my hurt. I am the one in bondage.*

4. If I forgive, I may get hurt again. *The truth is I am going to get hurt again by others regardless of what I do. So the issue is, "What is the best response?" to these upcoming hurts so that I am not living in fear and being controlled by others.*

5. If I ignore it, the problem will go away. *The problem just gets buried and resurfaces later. Unresolved baggage from the past is brought into the present.*

6. Revenge: the person has to pay for it. He needs to be punished and learn a lesson. I want to hang on to the right to be a judge. *I'm not God, and trying to play God will get me in trouble. Vengeance belongs to the Lord.*

7. Failure to understand God's love and forgiveness for me. *I cannot give a gift to someone unless I first have something to give.*

8. Seems too easy and unfair. It seems I'm overlooking or condoning his sin. *No, in fact I am charging and documenting the debt and recognizing that Jesus died on the cross for that sin.*

9. Waiting for the person to come to me first. *It rarely happens.*

10. The person isn't sorry for what he's done. *Chances are he'll never be sorry. Forgiveness is primarily for my benefit. I don't need to wait.*

11. If I choose to forgive, I'm acting like a hypocrite because I don't "feel" loving and forgiving. *The truth is I'm a hypocrite if I don't forgive because my real nature in Christ is now a forgiving nature.*

12. Waiting for a "convenient" time and a "feeling." *It will never be convenient. I will never "feel" like forgiving.*

13. Thinking it takes too much time. I don't have time to forgive. *I can't afford not to forgive. I am the one in torment and in suffering.*

14. Fear of feelings that might be stirred up. *God knows how to gently get out the feelings that need to be healed. I won't die or go crazy.*

The Performance Treadmill and Guilt - Day One

Goal: To understand the purpose of God's Law and to recognize how I might be
misusing it in my life.

1. Complete the following statements:

   God would be more pleased with me if . . .

   I would be a good/better Christian if I could . . .

   I feel God expects me to . . .

   God is disappointed with me when I . . .

   Your answers to these questions may reveal that you are still trying to be "good enough" to go to Heaven or to be loved and accepted by God.

   The Law (of the Old Testament) is an objective external standard that expresses the expectations of a righteous and holy God. Jesus summarized the Law with two commands: "Love the Lord your God" and "Love your neighbor as yourself." The Law reveals what this should look like in human behavior.

2. What do each of the following verses reveal concerning the purpose of God's Law?

   Now we recognize *and* know that the Law is good if any one uses it lawfully [for the purpose for which it was designed], Knowing *and* understanding this: that the Law is not enacted for the righteous (the upright and just, who are in right standing with God), but for the lawless and unruly, for the ungodly and sinful . . .   1 Timothy 1:8-9a Amplified

   What then was the purpose of the Law? It was added [later on, after the promise, to disclose and expose to men their guilt] because of transgressions *and* [to make men more conscious of the sinfulness] of sin.. . .   Galatians 3:19 Amplified

   So that the Law served [to us Jews] as our trainer [our guardian, our guide to Christ, to lead us] until Christ [came], that we might be justified (declared righteous, put in right standing with God) by *and* through faith.   Galatians 3:24 Amplified

> If you seek to be justified *and* declared righteous *and* to be given a right standing with God through the Law, you are brought to nothing *and* so separated (severed) from Christ. You have fallen away from grace (from God's gracious favor and unmerited blessing).
>
> Galatians 5:4 Amplified

The Law is not the Gospel. The Law was intended to be a "thermometer, not a thermostat." It reveals our standing in relationship to God's standards, but it does not make us capable of gaining or achieving those standards. The main purpose of the Law is to reveal to us God's holiness and our need of Him.

3. Read Romans 7:5-8.

What is aroused by the Law?

How are we released from the Law?

What does the Law show you?

The Gospel is the good news about God's grace in response to man's sin (failure to love God and others). The word "grace" means, "that which causes joy, pleasure, gratification, favor, acceptance. A favor done without expectation of return; the absolute freeness of the loving kindness of God to men finding its only motive in the bounty and benevolence of the Giver; unearned and unmerited favor." (Spiros Zodhiates, *The Complete Word Study Dictionary*)

> For it is by free grace (God's unmerited favor) that you are saved (delivered from judgment *and* made partakers of Christ's salvation) through [your] faith. And this [salvation] is not of yourselves [of your own doing, it came not through your own striving], but it is the gift of God; not because of works [not the fulfillment of the Law's demands], lest any man should boast. [It is not the result of what anyone can possibly do, so no one can pride himself in it or take glory to himself].
>
> Ephesians 2:8-9 Amplified

4. Spend a few minutes expressing gratitude to God for the free gift of salvation by personalizing and praying the verse above.

The Performance Treadmill and Guilt - Day Two

Goal: To evaluate how I'm trying to meet my needs for acceptance and approval and to receive God's acceptance and approval of me.

If you are already convinced that you are saved by grace and not through keeping the Law, can you still be living on the "performance treadmill?" You are if you are trying to gain approval and acceptance from God, others, or self through keeping the Law or standards.

1. To discover if this is true, look at question 1 of Day One. What do your answers reveal?

2. How are you trying or what are you trying to do to gain God's acceptance and approval?

3. In what areas do you feel unaccepted by God? Do you feel unaccepted because you have failed to keep God's commands or because you have believed a lie about yourself or God?

4. What do the following verses tell you about your acceptance and approval by God?

> Yet now has [Christ, the Messiah,] reconciled [you to God] in the body of His flesh through death, in order to present you holy and faultless and irreproachable in His [the Father's] presence.
>
> Colossians 1:22 Amplified

> Therefore, [there is] now no condemnation (no adjudging guilty of wrong) for those who are in Christ Jesus.
>
> Romans 8:1 Amplified

> Even as [in His love] He chose us - [actually picked us out for Himself as His own], in Christ before the foundation of the world; that we should be holy (consecrated and set apart for Him) and blameless in His sight, *even* above reproach, before Him in love.
>
> Ephesians 1:4 Amplified

> Wherefore, accept one another, just as Christ also accepted us to the glory of God.
>
> Romans 15:7 NAS

5. God's approval and acceptance of us is not based on our performance but on who we are: His Spirit-born children. Choose to accept by faith what God says in His Word and to receive God's approval and acceptance of you. Write Him a thank-you note.

The Performance Treadmill and Guilt - Day Three

Goal: To recognize any standards I am living by and learn what it means to walk by the Spirit.

Many times, we feel that we have to "stick to the rules" or "maintain certain standards" in order to make sure we live a Godly life and are accepted by others. We may fear that we will lose control of our life if we cease trying to achieve our standards. However, the truth is that living by self-imposed rules has absolutely no value in "restraining sensual indulgences" (the flesh). In fact, according to Romans 7, rules actually arouse sin!

> But sin, finding opportunity in the commandment [to express itself], got a hold on me and aroused and stimulated all kinds of forbidden desires (lust, covetousness). For without the Law sin is dead [the sense of it is inactive and a lifeless thing].
>
> Romans 7:8 Amplified

> For sin, seizing the opportunity and getting a hold on me [by taking its incentive] from the commandment, beguiled and entrapped and cheated me, and using it [as a weapon], killed me.
>
> Romans 7:11 Amplified

1. As you grew up, what were some of the family rules or standards (spoken or unspoken) that you were expected to live up to?

2. What are some of your church's standards that you feel you need to meet in order to be considered a "good Christian?"

3. List a standard you use to judge whether others are acceptable or worthy. (Hint: What are your pet peeves? When others don't conform, do you become angry?)

4. According to Colossians 2:20-23, living by standards and Laws appears to be beneficial, but actually has no profit (does not make us loving in our actions or attitudes). In your relationships, what are some of the negative consequences of living by the Law or standards?

5. Make a list of your standards that you have used to measure your worth or to gain acceptance. One by one, give your standards to God, acknowledging that living by your standards will never empower you to love God or others. Thank God that they are not His demands on you.

6. Ask God to teach you how to "walk by the Spirit" rather than walking in the "flesh" (living by Laws and standards). Meditate on the following verse and on what it means in your daily life. Write on a 3 x 5 card or sticky note, and put it where you will see it often.

> I have been crucified with Christ; and it is no longer I who live, but Christ lives in me; and the *life* which I now live in the flesh I live by faith in the Son of God, who loved me, and delivered Himself up for me. I do not nullify the grace of God; for if righteousness *comes* through the Law, then Christ died needlessly. Galatians 2:20-21 NAS

The Performance Treadmill and Guilt - Day Four

Goal: To discover the difference between living on the performance treadmill and living and walking in the freedom of the Spirit.

1. Read Galatians 3:2-3. What is your part in living by the Spirit?

    Rather than living by external rules, we are to live and walk by the Spirit, responding in faith to His inner prompting. "Walk" speaks of a continuous process, a moment-by-moment dependence on the Holy Spirit. Our part is to respond to His leading, and God's part is to empower us with His supernatural life.

2. Read the "Old Way of Law vs. New Way of Spirit" chart on pages 8.27-28 Note any old ways of living under the Law that apply to you. Ask God to begin to make the new way of the Spirit your experience.

Jesus invites all who are tired, exhausted, and frustrated from trying to live the "Christian" life by their own efforts to come to Him and rest. The word "rest" means to cease from living the Christian life by self-effort. It is putting our faith in Jesus and allowing Him to live His life through us.

> Come to Me, all you who labor and are heavy-laden *and* overburdened, and I will cause you to rest. [I will ease and relieve and refresh your souls.] Take My yoke upon you and learn of Me, for I am gentle (meek) and humble (lowly) in heart, and you will find rest (relief and ease and refreshment and recreation and blessed quiet) for your souls. For My yoke is wholesome (useful, good—not harsh, hard, sharp, or pressing, but comfortable, gracious, and pleasant), and My burden is light *and* easy to be borne.
>
> Matthew 11:28-30 Amplified

3. List some of your "red flags" (indicators) that tell you that you are not "resting" in Jesus (trusting Him to live through you).

    Examples:
    *   When I become anxious and stressed about all I have to do.
    *   When I think that God is disgusted or disappointed with me for some failure in my life (and I feel shame and condemnation).

4. For each of the examples you listed above, describe how you could "rest" in Jesus?

Examples:
- When I am stressed, cast all my worries on Him. Give Him my list of things to do, as well as my expectations, and trust Him to empower me and direct my day.
- When I fail, agree with God concerning my sin and thank Him that He has not only forgiven me, but made me acceptable. Choose to renew my mind with the truth about my new identity and trust the Holy Spirit to empower me to do what is right.

5. Look back at your answers on page 1.11, Day One of "Discovering the Root of Our Problems." In what ways are the problem(s) you described a result of living by your own standards or self-effort instead of relying on the Holy Spirit?

6. Personalize Matthew 11:28-30 as your prayer, trusting in Jesus to give you rest from your self-effort and to empower you through His Spirit.

Example:
"Jesus, I am tired and weary of trying to do things for You and trying to please others. Thank You Jesus for inviting me to come to You to find rest. I am exhausted from trying to live the Christian life through self-effort. Teach me what it means to rest in You and depend on Your Spirit in my daily life."

The Performance Treadmill and Guilt - Day Five

Goal: To recognize and heal emotional guilt.

1. Check below the symptoms of emotional guilt which you recognize in your life.
    Write one reason why you feel guilty and how you experience this guilt.

❑   Self-condemnation: the constant blaming of oneself. This can lead to depression.

❑   Self-punishment: any form of punishment which is inflicted upon oneself, usually to pay for some wrongdoing.

❑   Depression: The end result of guilt that hasn't been addressed.

❑   Sense of Disapproval: The result of expectations of yourself or others that have not been met.

❑   Physical Symptoms: can include headaches, fatigue, and insomnia.

❑   Rationalization: an attempt to justify one's actions to counter guilt feelings.

❑   Compensation: An attempt to soothe the conscience by doing things considered to be good. Another attempt to counter guilt feelings.

❑   Anger: A feeling of hostility toward those who seem to prompt guilt feelings.

❑   "Goody Two-Shoes:" Exemplary behavior which is often another attempt to mask internal guilt feelings.

❑   Fear and Dread: Two closely related emotions which are often associated with unresolved guilt feelings.

2. For each example you wrote above, confess (agree with God; give thanks) concerning His complete forgiveness of you and for giving you the righteousness of Christ.

The Performance Treadmill and Guilt - Lesson Eight

Name _____ Date _____

Answer the following questions. To turn in page to small group leader, use identical perforated page in back of book.

1. How is living on the "Performance Treadmill" evident in your life?

2. What laws or standards have you tried to live up to in order to earn God's approval and acceptance? What has been the result of living by these laws or standards?

3. What standards have you tried to live up to in order to gain a sense of self-worth or to get approval and acceptance from others?

4. How has living on the "Performance Treadmill" affected the quality of your life? Your relationship with God? With others?

5. What is your understanding of how you are to live the Christian life?

6. Mark the graph to indicate how much of this week's assignment you completed.

None	50%	100%

Record Your Prayer Requests:

Old Way of Law vs. New Way of Spirit

Old Way of Law

New Way of Spirit

1. External Code
The moral precepts of God are only an external code of conduct. The Law commands obedience but provides no inclination or desire to obey.

1. Internal Desire
The moral precepts of God are written on our hearts. The Spirit prompts us in our thoughts and gives us a desire to obey.

2. Commanding
The Law commands obedience but gives no enabling power.

2. Enabling
The Spirit empowers us to obey the law of love.

3. Hostility
Because of our hostility to God's Law before becoming a Christian, the Law's commands actually provoke and incite our flesh to sin.

3. Delight
The Spirit, by removing our hostility, giving us a new spirit and writing the Law on our hearts, causes us to delight in God's Law.

4. Fear
The Law produces a legalistic response to God. We try to obey because we fear punishment for disobedience or we hope to win favor with God.

4. Gratitude
The Spirit, by showing us God's grace, produces a response of love and gratitude. We obey, not out of fear or to earn favor, but out of gratitude for favor already given.

5. Working
Under the Law, we perform in order to be accepted by God. Because our performance is always imperfect, we never feel completely accepted by Him. We live from a position of weakness, because we work to be accepted, but never achieve it.

5. Relying
The Spirit bears witness with our spirit that we are accepted by God through the merit of Christ. By relying solely on His perfect righteousness, we know we are accepted by Him. We live from a position of strength, because we have been made acceptable.

Old Way of Law	New Way of Spirit

6. Principles

Under the Law we live by principles and rely on our knowledge and self-discipline. This is reliance upon the natural cause and effect.

6. Promises

Living by the Spirit is living by the promises of God and relying on the Holy Spirit. Living by the Spirit requires faith in the supernatural.

7. Striving

Living under the Law creates pressure to perform in order to earn God's blessing and acceptance. Because we cannot keep God's Law, we never feel accepted by God.

7. Resting

Living by the Spirit brings freedom to rest in the faithfulness of God who has already blessed us with every spiritual blessing. It is trusting in Christ's perfect life within to live a life pleasing to God.

8. Persecution

Those who live under the Law tend to persecute and judge those around them for not keeping the Law.

8. Blessing

Those who live by the Spirit understand the grace of God and extend it to others. They bless others with God's unconditional love and acceptance.

9. We Are Responsible

Under the old covenant of the Law we were responsible to obey the Law in order to receive God's promised blessing. Failure to keep the Law brings a curse.

9. God Takes Initiative

Under the new covenant God takes the initiative and responsibility for living the Christian life through us. Our part is to live by faith and God's part is to conform us to Christ.

10. Performance Consciousness

Living by the Law creates a performance consciousness, focusing on self. This drains us of spiritual life and robs us of joy and peace.

10. God Consciousness

Living by the Spirit creates a God consciousness, focusing on who He is and what He has done for us. This causes us to love and worship God, resulting in joy and peace in our life.

11. Failure

Living by the Law leads to further sin and failure because we are walking in the flesh.

11. Victory

Walking by the Spirit produces freedom and victory over sin and the fruit of the Spirit is produced in our life.

A Life Transformed - Day One

Goal: To recognize how my response to my problems reveals my view of God.

1. Read over the funnel chart explanation.

2. Funnel a present situation that you are struggling with using the blank funnel provided.

USING THE "FUNNEL CHART"

Ask the Holy Spirit to guide your thoughts. Complete the left side of the funnel chart in regard to the feelings and actions in your life. Begin by thinking of a situation that really bothered you this past week or month.

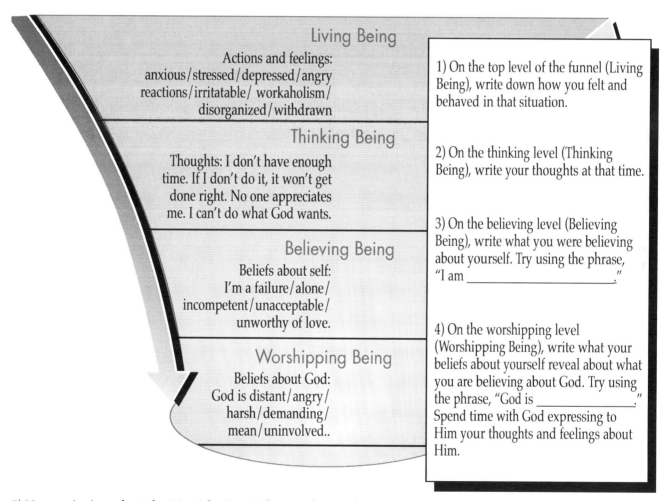

Living Being
Actions and feelings:
anxious/stressed/depressed/angry
reactions/irritatable/ workaholism/
disorganized/withdrawn

Thinking Being
Thoughts: I don't have enough
time. If I don't do it, it won't get
done right. No one appreciates
me. I can't do what God wants.

Believing Being
Beliefs about self:
I'm a failure/alone/
incompetent/unacceptable/
unworthy of love.

Worshipping Being
Beliefs about God:
God is distant/angry/
harsh/demanding/
mean/uninvolved..

1) On the top level of the funnel (Living Being), write down how you felt and behaved in that situation.

2) On the thinking level (Thinking Being), write your thoughts at that time.

3) On the believing level (Believing Being), write what you were believing about yourself. Try using the phrase, "I am _____."

4) On the worshipping level (Worshipping Being), write what your beliefs about yourself reveal about what you are believing about God. Try using the phrase, "God is _____." Spend time with God expressing to Him your thoughts and feelings about Him.

5) Now, go back up the right side of the funnel chart. At the worshipping level, contrast your negative beliefs about God to what is true about Him. Give Scripture references. Stop and reject the lies you have been believing about God, and thank Him for Who He really is. (You may not feel this yet, but it is true nevertheless.) Refer to page 4.22 for truths about God relating to us and pages 4.16-4.17 for characteristics of God.

6) On the believing level, write what is true about you in light of God's Word and His character. (See "Creating a Christian Identity" page 3.13.) Acknowledge to God the lies you have been believing about yourself, and replace the lies with the truth.

7) On the thinking level, write what thoughts will result from your new beliefs about God and yourself.

8) On the living level, write what behaviors will result from your new beliefs about God and yourself. Your feelings will eventually follow. Ask the Holy Spirit what step of faith (an action, belief to accept, attitude to be willing to change, etc.) He wants you to take.

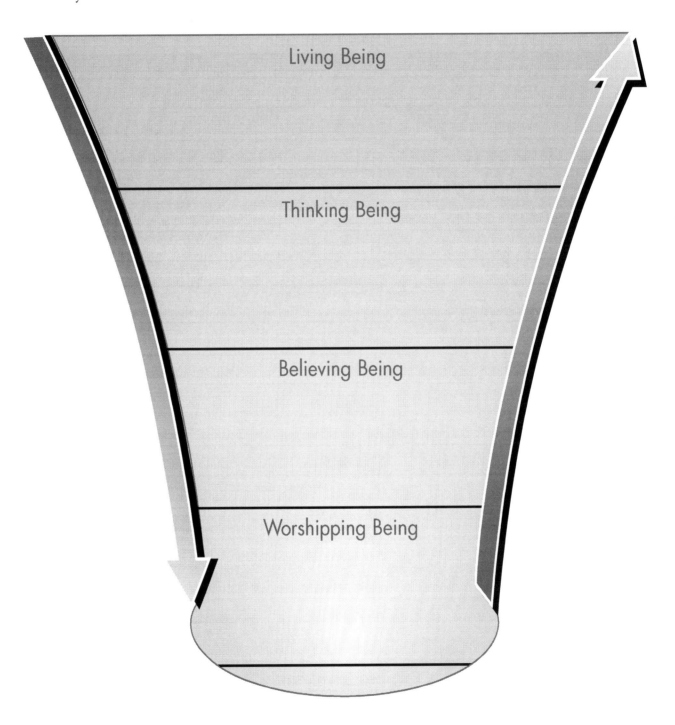

A Life Transformed - Day Two

Goal: To recognize how God wants to make Himself personally known to you in the midst of life's problems.

1. Look back to "Summary" at the end of each lesson. List the ones about which God has given you a greater understanding.

2. What changes are resulting from your new understanding of these truths?

3. Read over "Problem Solving in Light of Who God Is" on the next page and then list the characteristics of God that He wants to reveal to you through your present problems.

4. Spend time worshipping God for Who He is.

PROBLEM SOLVING IN LIGHT OF WHO GOD IS

GOD IS COMPASSIONATE - He cares about all of my problems, and He cares about me. He feels my pain. (2 Corinthians 1:3; 1 Peter 5:7).

GOD IS OMNIPOTENT - He is able to solve my problems. Nothing is too hard for Him, and no problem is too big. Through Him I can do all things (Philippians 4:13).

GOD IS OMNISCIENT - He knows all about my problems, and He knows the solution. He has already planned to work these problems together for my good (Romans 8:28-29).

GOD IS WISE - He allowed this problem in my life because He knows what is best for me, and He also knows the best solution.

GOD IS OMNIPRESENT - As I face problems, He is with me and in me. He never asks me to solve problems by myself. The living God is my Helper (Isaiah 41:10; Matthew 28:20; Hebrews 13:5,6).

GOD IS IMMUTABLE (NEVER CHANGING) - The same God Who saved me (solved my biggest problem) is able to help me in whatever problem I face. The God Who helped David, Daniel, Paul, etc., in their problems is the same God Who is able to help me. I can always count on God being God (Hebrews 13:8).

GOD IS SOVEREIGN - He is in complete control of the situation. He allowed this problem to come into my life. Both my problem and I are in His loving hands.

GOD IS FAITHFUL - As I trust God for the solution to this problem, He will not fail me. His promises cannot fail. I can rely on God in this situation. God is absolutely trustworthy, dependable, and reliable. (2 Corinthians 1:20)

GOD IS TRUE - I can trust God's promises in His Word because God does not and cannot lie! What He says He will do, He will do! (Numbers 23:19; Titus 1:2)

GOD IS ETERNAL - As I view my problems in light of eternity, they become quite insignificant (Deuteronomy 33:27; 2 Corinthians 4:17).

GOD IS GOOD - In the midst of my problems and difficulties, God wants to bless me. He wants to make me more like Jesus (Romans 8:28-29).

GOD IS RIGHTEOUS - In allowing these problems to come into my life, God did what was right. God makes no mistakes!

GOD IS LOVE - God wants to reveal His love to me through these problems. There is no problem, no matter how great, that can separate me from His love (Romans 8:35-39).

GOD IS JUST - God is absolutely just in all that He does, including allowing these problems in my life.

GOD IS IN THE MIDST OF PRESSURES AND PROBLEMS! (Exodus 33:14; Deuteronomy 4:29-31; 31:8; Isaiah 43:10-11).

A Life Transformed - Day Three

Goal: To identify areas where you need to grow in understanding and faith.

1. Read over the "Summary" at the end of each lesson. List the key points which you do not fully understand.

2. Spend some time asking God to help you understand them.

A Life Transformed - Day Four

Goal: To review what God has taught you through these lessons.

1. What did God identify as one of the major root problem(s) in your life?

2. What corrupted beliefs did God reveal to you?

3. How has your perspective of yourself changed?

4. How has your perspective of God changed?

5. How has your perspective of living the Christian life changed?

6. What are some lies the enemy uses against you to rob you of joy and peace?

7. What truth have you learned to combat these schemes?

8. What is your part in building an intimate relationship with God?

9. Spend a few minutes thanking God for all that He has taught you and for the changes you see Him making in your life.

A Life Transformed - Day Five

Goal: To make a plan for continuing to renew your mind with God's truth.

1. Read through "Additional Helps for the Renewing Process" on the next page. Check the ones that stand out to you as possible future assignments.

2. Of those you checked, with which will you start? Schedule a time to get started.

3. Which of the assignments you checked needs to be an ongoing lifestyle change? Ask the Holy Spirit to motivate, empower, and remind you to implement these changes.

Additional Helps for the Renewing Process

What you have learned and applied in these nine lessons is only the beginning of the renewal process. The following are some suggestions to help you continue on in this process.

1. Read the Bible with the single purpose of seeing Who God is. It is helpful to start with a Bible that has not been written in, and with a color highlighter, highlight each verse that reveals something about the character of God. Start in the Gospels and then go to the Psalms (John is an excellent place to start).

2. Keep a personal notebook to record the lies that God reveals to you that need to be put off and the truth that needs to be put on. This will be a good reference tool when encountering future problems.

3. Practice meditating on the Truth and "Truth talk." Meditating simply means "to think about something." Truth-talking is the practice of telling yourself the Truth and praying the Truth back to God. Psalm 23 is a good example of this type of prayer. Start by praying back Scripture, personalizing it in your own words.

4. Develop the habit of meditating on the Truth by writing down a specific helpful Truth on a 3 x 5 card and carrying this with you. Connect meditating on this Truth with another repetitive practice, such as getting a drink, eating a meal, or going to the bathroom. Soon you will have the Truth cemented into your thinking.

5. Take the FatherGod Test in the "FatherCare" booklet. Write on 3x5 index cards the characteristics of God for which your faith is the weakest. As needs or fears arise, practice Truth-talking about God as your Father.

6. Continue to practice putting off the lies you have believed about yourself as instructed in the handout, "Creating a Christian Identity" (page 3.28). Use one of the methods mentioned in #4 and #5.

7. Practice keeping a REED journal (see week six: Controlling Emotions). Be sure to record the date and circumstances that prompted the negative feelings. This will help you recognize if there is a pattern to these negative emotions. Be sure to work all the way through REED to the "evaluate" and "decide" steps; otherwise, all you will accomplish is obtaining a little relief from suppressing your emotions. Record the lies you have believed and the truth from God's perspective.

8. Make worship a lifestyle. Pray Scripture back to God. Sing songs of praise and worship to God. Practice "doing" the Psalms instead of just reading them. Listen to and sing along with praise and worship music. This will help you focus on God instead of yourself and your circumstances. Talk to God about everything, as you would your closest friend.

9. Read Christian books and listen to teaching tapes that will reinforce the truth that you have learned through this workbook. Look over the Suggested Reading list (page 9.25) and check the books that would help reinforce the truths you need to focus on. You cannot hear the truth too much. Remember how long you have listened to the lies.

10. Fellowship with other believers who are seeking to know God and grow in their new identity. It is imperative that you stay connected and involved with people in the Body of Christ who will pray for you and encourage you in your faith. Standing alone against your three-fold enemy is very difficult.

11. Remember, your goal is to know God experientially in the midst of life's problems and to allow God to transform you into Christ-likeness. To "seek first the kingdom of God and His righteousness" begins by receiving God's unconditional love for you. Make it a habit to spend a few minutes several times each day receiving God's love. This is not a time of Bible study or prayer but a time to be still and know that He is God and to receive His love by faith.

12. Share with others what God is teaching you and what He is doing in your life. Giving to others what God has freely given you will reinforce the truth in your own life.

13. Daily practice consciously and verbally yielding your expectations and rights to God. Trust Him to meet your needs in the very best way and at the right time.

14. Practice asking yourself and God two questions: What is God doing in my life? What does He want me to do? Expect God to speak to you through His Word and through His indwelling Spirit. We do not have to live in continual confusion or bondage. When you have trouble discerning the answer to these two questions, talk to someone whom you respect for his walk with God. None of us hears God perfectly all the time. That's why we need to stay connected to the Body.

15. Reread the lessons in this workbook, and work through the specific assignments that address your particular needs.

Remember that this is an ongoing, moment-by-moment, lifelong process.

A Life Transformed - Lesson Nine

Name _____ Date _____

Answer the following questions. To turn in page to small group leader, use identical perforated page in back of book.

1. What has been the most significant thing God has revealed to you through this nine-week study?

2. How has this truth begun to change your life?

3. How has God worked in your life during your Discovery Group experience?

4. What is one area of your life in which you would like to experience transformation?

5. Mark the graph to indicate how much of this week's assignment you completed.

None	50%	100%

Record Your Prayer Requests:

Discovery Group Guidelines

1. Time

Every effort will be made to start and end on time. Do your best to be on time.

2. Confidentiality

We all need to feel free to express ourselves openly without the fear of being discussed later, even by other group members; therefore nothing said in this group leaves this group. When you discuss your group experiences with a friend or spouse, share only what you gained or learned. Do not share anyone's experiences but your own. Do not share any names, descriptions or occupations of group members, etc., with people outside the group. During the week, do not discuss any other group members, even among yourselves.

3. Communication with each other

- Don't try to "fix" anyone else
- Use "I" statements, not "you" statements
- Follow Ephesians 4:29; "Do not let any unwholesome talk come out of your mouths, but only what is helpful for building others up according to their needs, that it may benefit those who listen."

4. Participation

This will make your group time more meaningful for you and for everyone else as you share your thoughts, experiences and feelings. We will all benefit from one another, so don't deprive others of your input. However, in the spirit of James 5:16 ("therefore, confess your sins to one another, and pray for one another, so that you may be healed."), share only your own sins or weaknesses, not those of others.

5. Attendance

Each member's attendance is very important. Your absence affects the dynamics of the group, therefore, give the group meeting a high priority. If you cannot attend, please call and inform your group leader prior to the meeting.

6. Homework

The daily assignments are intended to help you interact with God each day concerning your individual needs and problems. Change and healing are possible only when we allow God to be involved in our daily lives. Each assignment will usually require about 20-30 minutes.

Discovery Group Covenant

To encourage a high level of trust, love, and openness in my discovery group, I, _____, covenant with my group's other members to do the following:

- I will make attendance at each group session a priority for the next agreed number of weeks. During these weeks, I will choose this group first when making decisions about my priorities and my time.

- I will commit my time each week to complete the appropriate assignments before the group session.

- I will keep confidential all information group members share. I will not share matters from the group with any outside person or mention the information as a prayer concern. I understand that breaking the confidentiality of the group could result in being asked to leave the group.

- I will support the other group members in their desire to grow emotionally and spiritually by encouraging them to evaluate honestly their beliefs and behavior.

- I will be honest about my own feelings and emotions as I participate in the group.

- I will be patient with other group members as we allow God to work in each of our lives. I will not try to give advice or to pressure other group members to do what I think best.

- I will inform my group leader of any physical or emotional problems that might arise and prohibit my participation in the group.

Signed: _____ Date: _____

_____   _____

_____   _____

_____   _____

_____   _____

Discovering the Root of Our Problems - Lesson One

Name _____ Date _____

Answer the following questions. To turn in page to small group leader, use identical perforated page in back of book.

1. Briefly describe from DAY ONE the problem with which you are presently struggling.

2. What are some of your "beliefs" that relate to your area of struggle?

3. How are these beliefs affecting you (emotionally, relationally, behaviorally)?

4. What is God showing you from this week's lesson?

5. How often do you turn to God's Word for answers to your problems?
___never   ___seldom   ___often   ___ very often   ___ always

6. What questions do you have concerning this week's assignment?

7. Mark the graph to indicate how much of this week's assignment you completed.

None	50%	100%

Record Your Prayer Requests:

Understanding the Good News - Lesson Two

Name_____Date_____

Answer the following questions. To turn in page to small group leader, use identical perforated page in back of book.

1. What has your understanding of salvation been before this lesson?

2. What new understanding of the "good news" did you gain from this lesson?

3. When did you personally believe the "good news" and receive eternal life?

4. Is there anything you have done that you believe God has not forgiven? If so, what?

5. How confident are you of God's presence in your daily life?

6. What wrong beliefs did you recognize from this week's lesson?

7. Mark the graph to indicate how much of this week's assignment you completed.

| None | 50% | 100% |

Record Your Prayer Requests:

Seeing Ourselves As God Sees Us - Lesson Three

Name _____ Date _____

Answer the following questions. To turn in page to small group leader, use identical perforated page in back of book.

1. According to what you have learned about the nature of man, what changed in you at salvation?

2. How does understanding that you have a new nature give you confidence concerning your salvation and spiritual growth?

3. What wrong beliefs about yourself do you need to put off?

4. How would believing your new identity and relying on the Holy Spirit in your daily life affect the way you respond to your present problems?

5. What questions do you have concerning the nature of man and your new identity?

6. Mark the graph to indicate how much of this week's assignment you completed.

None	50%	100%

Record Your Prayer Requests:

Getting to Know Our Heavenly Father - Lesson Four

Name _____ Date _____

Answer the following questions. To turn in page to small group leader, use identical perforated page in back of book.

1. What corrupted beliefs about God as Father did you recognize through this lesson?

2. How would knowing and relating to God as your Father affect your life (emotionally, relationally, behaviorally)?

3. How would relating to God as an unconditionally loving and perfect Father affect your life?

4. What from this week's assignment was most meaningful to you?

5. What characteristic(s) of God need strengthening in your life?

6. Mark the graph to indicate how much of this week's assignment you completed.

| None | 50% | 100% |

Record Your Prayer Requests:

Living By the Spirit - Lesson Five

Name _____ Date _____

Answer the following questions. To turn in page to small group leader, use identical perforated page in back of book.

1. What encouraged you most about this week's study on the Holy Spirit?

2. List any fears or concerns you have about surrendering control of your life to the Holy Spirit.

3. What do you feel would keep God from filling you with His Spirit?

4. How would living by the Spirit affect your life and your current struggles?

5. Mark the graph to indicate how much of this week's assignment you completed.

None	50%	100%

Record Your Prayer Requests:

Controlling Emotions - Lesson Six

Name _____ Date _____

Answer the following questions. To turn in page to small group leader, use identical perforated page in back of book.

1. What negative emotion did you experience most this past week? What kind of thoughts usually produced this emotion?

2. What did these thoughts tell you about what you were believing?

3. What new insight or perspective did God give you when you expressed your feelings honestly to Him?

4. How will practicing REED improve your relationship with God and your quality of life?

5. Mark the graph to indicate how much of this week's assignment you completed.

None	50%	100%

Record Your Prayer Requests:

Expectations, Anger, and Bitterness - Lesson Seven

Name _____ Date _____

Answer the following questions. To turn in page to small group leader, use identical perforated page in back of book.

1. About what have you been the most angry?

2. What expectations or rights are you holding onto that are contributing to this anger?

3. How are unforgiveness and bitterness affecting your life and relationships?

4. Have you forgiven those who have hurt you? If not, what do you think are the obstacles to forgiving them?

5. Whom did God lead you to forgive through this assignment?

6. Mark the graph to indicate how much of this week's assignment you completed.

None	50%	100%

Record Your Prayer Requests:

The Performance Treadmill and Guilt - Lesson Eight

Name _____ Date _____

Answer the following questions. To turn in page to small group leader, use identical perforated page in back of book.

1. How is living on the "Performance Treadmill" evident in your life?

2. What laws or standards have you tried to live up to in order to earn God's approval and acceptance? What has been the result of living by these laws or standards?

3. What standards have you tried to live up to in order to gain a sense of self-worth or to get approval and acceptance from others?

4. How has living on the "Performance Treadmill" affected the quality of your life? Your relationship with God? With others?

5. What is your understanding of how you are to live the Christian life?

6. Mark the graph to indicate how much of this week's assignment you completed.

None	50%	100%

Record Your Prayer Requests:

A Life Transformed - Lesson Nine

Name _____ Date _____

Answer the following questions. To turn in page to small group leader, use identical perforated page in back of book.

1. What has been the most significant thing God has revealed to you through this nine-week study?

2. How has this truth begun to change your life?

3. How has God worked in your life during your Discovery Group experience?

4. What is one area of your life in which you would like to experience transformation?

5. Mark the graph to indicate how much of this week's assignment you completed.

None	50%	100%

Record Your Prayer Requests:

Made in the USA
Lexington, KY
13 February 2014